The Latest UK Air Fryer

Cookbook for Beginners

1000 Days Super-Easy and Delicious Air Fryer Recipes That Anyone Can Learn Easily Incl. Side Dishes, Desserts, Snacks and More

Sydnie Hackett

Warning-Disclaimer

The purpose of this book is to educate and entertain. The author or publisher does not guarantee that anyone following the techniques, suggestions, tips, ideas, or strategies will become successful. The author and publisher shall have neither liability or responsibility to anyone with respect to any loss or damage caused, or alleged to be caused, directly or indirectly by the information contained in this book

Table of Contents

Chapter 5 Beef, Pork, and Lamb   24

Chapter 6 Fish and Seafood   33

Chapter 8 Vegetables and Sides

Chapter 9 Vegetarian Mains

Chapter 10 Desserts

INTRODUCTION

My fellow foodies, I am thrilled to share with you my new cookbook filled with delicious recipes made exclusively for air fryers!

I have always loved experimenting with different kitchen appliances, but the air fryer has quickly become one of my favorites. It's an appliance that allows you to enjoy all your favorite fried foods with less oil, less mess, and a shorter cooking time.

This cookbook is designed to be user-friendly, so whether you are an experienced chef or just getting started in the kitchen, you'll find something to love. I've included a variety of recipes, from traditional comfort foods to healthy alternatives, and some innovative dishes that you might not expect to cook in an air fryer.

Cooking with an air fryer is also a fun and interactive experience. You can experiment with different ingredients and seasonings to create your own unique twists on classic recipes. And the best part? You can indulge in all the fried foods you love without the guilt.

Throughout the cookbook, I've included tips and tricks to make the most out of your air fryer. You'll learn about different cooking techniques, how to properly clean and maintain your appliance, and how to use accessories to take your cooking to the next level.

I hope this cookbook inspires you to try new recipes, get creative in the kitchen, and most importantly, have fun! With this cookbook and your air fryer, the possibilities are endless. Let's get cooking!

Chapter 1 Breakfasts

Chapter 1 Breakfasts

Breakfast Pitta

Prep time: 5 minutes | Cook time: 6 minutes | Serves 2

1 wholemeal pitta
2 teaspoons olive oil
½ shallot, diced
¼ teaspoon garlic, minced
1 large egg
¼ teaspoon dried oregano
¼ teaspoon dried thyme
⅛ teaspoon salt
2 tablespoons shredded Parmesan cheese

1. Preheat the air fryer to 192°C. 2. Brush the top of the pitta with olive oil, then spread the diced shallot and minced garlic over the pitta. 3. Crack the egg into a small bowl or ramekin, and season it with oregano, thyme, and salt. 4. Place the pitta into the air fryer basket, and gently pour the egg onto the top of the pitta. Sprinkle with cheese over the top. 5. Bake for 6 minutes. 6. Allow to cool for 5 minutes before cutting into pieces for serving.

Bacon, Broccoli and Cheese Bread Pudding

Prep time: 30 minutes | Cook time: 48 minutes | Serves 2 to 4

230 g thick cut bacon, cut into ¼-inch pieces
700 ml brioche bread or rolls, cut into ½-inch cubes
3 eggs
235 ml milk
½ teaspoon salt
freshly ground black pepper
235 ml frozen broccoli florets, thawed and chopped
350 ml grated Swiss cheese

1. Preheat the air fryer to 204°C. 2. Air fry the bacon for 6 to 10 minutes until crispy, shaking the basket a few times while it cooks to help it cook evenly. Remove the bacon and set it aside on a paper towel. 3. Air fry the brioche bread cubes for 2 minutes to dry and toast lightly. (If your brioche is a few days old and slightly stale, you can omit this step.) 4. Butter a cake pan. Combine all the ingredients in a large bowl and toss well. Transfer the mixture to the buttered cake pan, cover with aluminum foil and refrigerate the bread pudding overnight, or for at least 8 hours. 5. Remove the casserole from the refrigerator an hour before you plan to cook, and let it sit on the countertop to come to room temperature. 6. Preheat the air fryer to 166°C. Transfer the covered cake pan, to the basket of the air fryer, lowering the dish into the basket using a sling made of aluminum foil (fold a piece of aluminum foil into a strip about 2-inches wide by 24-inches long). Fold the ends of the aluminum foil over the top of the dish before returning the basket to the air fryer. Air fry for 20 minutes. Remove the foil and air fry for an additional 20 minutes. If the top starts to brown a little too much before the custard has set, simply return the foil to the pan. The bread pudding has cooked through when a skewer inserted into the center comes out clean.

Cheddar-Ham-Corn Muffins

Prep time: 10 minutes | Cook time: 6 to 8 minutes per batch | Makes 8 muffins

180 ml cornmeal/polenta
60 ml flour
1½ teaspoons baking powder
¼ teaspoon salt
1 egg, beaten
2 tablespoons rapeseed oil
120 ml milk
120 ml shredded sharp Cheddar cheese
120 ml diced ham
8 foil muffin cups, liners removed and sprayed with cooking spray

1. Preheat the air fryer to 200°C. 2. In a medium bowl, stir together the cornmeal, flour, baking powder, and salt. 3. Add egg, oil, and milk to dry ingredients and mix well. 4. Stir in shredded cheese and diced ham. 5. Divide batter among the muffin cups. 6. Place 4 filled muffin cups in air fryer basket and bake for 5 minutes. 7. Reduce temperature to 166°C and bake for 1 to 2 minutes or until toothpick inserted in center of muffin comes out clean. 8. Repeat steps 6 and 7 to cook remaining muffins.

Golden Avocado Tempura

Prep time: 5 minutes | Cook time: 10 minutes | Serves 4

120 ml bread crumbs
½ teaspoons salt
1 Haas avocado, pitted, peeled
and sliced
Liquid from 1 can white beans

1. Preheat the air fryer to 176°C. 2. Mix the bread crumbs and salt in a shallow bowl until well-incorporated. 3. Dip the avocado slices in the bean liquid, then into the bread crumbs. 4. Put the avocados in the air fryer, taking care not to overlap any slices, and air fry for 10 minutes, giving the basket a good shake at the halfway point. 5. Serve immediately.

Turkey Sausage Breakfast Pizza

Prep time: 15 minutes | Cook time: 24 minutes | Serves 2

4 large eggs, divided	120 ml shredded low-moisture
1 tablespoon water	Mozzarella or other melting
½ teaspoon garlic powder	cheese
½ teaspoon onion granules	1 link cooked turkey sausage,
½ teaspoon dried oregano	chopped (about 60 g)
2 tablespoons coconut flour	2 sun-dried tomatoes, finely
3 tablespoons grated Parmesan	chopped
cheese	2 spring onions, thinly sliced

1. Preheat the air fryer to 204°C. Line a cake pan with parchment paper and lightly coat the paper with olive oil. 2. In a large bowl, whisk 2 of the eggs with the water, garlic powder, onion granules, and dried oregano. Add the coconut flour, breaking up any lumps with your hands as you add it to the bowl. Stir the coconut flour into the egg mixture, mixing until smooth. Stir in the Parmesan cheese. Allow the mixture to rest for a few minutes until thick and dough-like. 3. Transfer the mixture to the prepared pan. Use a spatula to spread it evenly and slightly up the sides of the pan. Air fry until the crust is set but still light in color, about 10 minutes. Top with the cheeses, sausage, and sun-dried tomatoes. 4. Break the remaining 2 eggs into a small bowl, then slide them onto the pizza. Return the pizza to the air fryer. Air fry 10 to 14 minutes until the egg whites are set and the yolks are the desired doneness. Top with the scallions and allow to rest for 5 minutes before serving.

Wholemeal Blueberry Muffins

Prep time: 10 minutes | Cook time: 15 minutes | Serves 6

Olive oil cooking spray	350 ml plus 1 tablespoon
120 ml unsweetened applesauce	wholemeal, divided
60 ml honey	½ teaspoon baking soda
120 ml non-fat plain Greek	½ teaspoon baking powder
yoghurt	½ teaspoon salt
1 teaspoon vanilla extract	120 ml blueberries, fresh or
1 large egg	frozen

1. Preheat the air fryer to 182°C. Lightly coat the inside of six silicone muffin cups or a six-cup muffin tin with olive oil cooking spray. 2. In a large bowl, combine the applesauce, honey, yoghurt, vanilla, and egg and mix until smooth. 3. Sift in 350 ml of the flour, the baking soda, baking powder, and salt into the wet mixture, then stir until just combined. 4. In a small bowl, toss the blueberries with the remaining 1 tablespoon flour, then fold the mixture into the muffin batter. 5. Divide the mixture evenly among the prepared muffin cups and place into the basket of the air fryer. Bake for 12 to 15 minutes, or until golden brown on top and a toothpick inserted into the middle of one of the muffins comes out clean. 6. Allow to cool for 5 minutes before serving.

Gold Avocado

Prep time: 5 minutes | Cook time: 6 minutes | Serves 4

2 large avocados, sliced	120 ml flour
¼ teaspoon paprika	2 eggs, beaten
Salt and ground black pepper,	235 ml bread crumbs
to taste	

1. Preheat the air fryer to 204°C. 2. Sprinkle paprika, salt and pepper on the slices of avocado. 3. Lightly coat the avocados with flour. Dredge them in the eggs, before covering with bread crumbs. 4. Transfer to the air fryer and air fry for 6 minutes. 5. Serve warm.

Fried Chicken Wings with Waffles

Prep time: 10 minutes | Cook time: 30 minutes | Serves 4

8 whole chicken wings	120 ml plain flour
1 teaspoon garlic powder	Cooking oil spray
Chicken seasoning, for	8 frozen waffles
preparing the chicken	Pure maple syrup, for serving
Freshly ground black pepper, to	(optional)
taste	

1. In a medium bowl, combine the chicken and garlic powder and season with chicken seasoning and pepper. Toss to coat. 2. Transfer the chicken to a resealable plastic bag and add the flour. Seal the bag and shake it to coat the chicken thoroughly. 3. Insert the crisper plate into the basket and the basket into the unit. Preheat the unit by selecting AIR FRY, setting the temperature to 204°C, and setting the time to 3 minutes. Select START/STOP to begin. 4. Once the unit is preheated, spray the crisper plate with cooking oil. Using tongs, transfer the chicken from the bag to the basket. It is okay to stack the chicken wings on top of each other. Spray them with cooking oil. 5. Select AIR FRY, set the temperature to 204°C, and set the time to 20 minutes. Select START/STOP to begin. 6. After 5 minutes, remove the basket and shake the wings. Reinsert the basket to resume cooking. Remove and shake the basket every 5 minutes until the chicken is fully cooked. 7. When the cooking is complete, remove the cooked chicken from the basket; cover to keep warm. 8. Rinse the basket and crisper plate with warm water. Insert them back into the unit. 9. Select AIR FRY, set the temperature to 182°C, and set the time to 3 minutes. Select START/STOP to begin. 10. Once the unit is preheated, spray the crisper plate with cooking spray. Working in batches, place the frozen waffles into the basket. Do not stack them. Spray the waffles with cooking oil. 11. Select AIR FRY, set the temperature to 182°C, and set the time to 6 minutes. Select START/STOP to begin. 12. When the cooking is complete, repeat steps 10 and 11 with the remaining waffles. 13. Serve the waffles with the chicken and a touch of maple syrup, if desired.

Sausage and Egg Breakfast Burrito

Prep time: 5 minutes | Cook time: 30 minutes | Serves 6

6 eggs	(removed from casings)
Salt and pepper, to taste	120 ml salsa
Cooking oil	6 medium (8-inch) flour tortillas
120 ml chopped red pepper	120 ml shredded Cheddar
120 ml chopped green pepper	cheese
230 g chicken sausage meat	

1. In a medium bowl, whisk the eggs. Add salt and pepper to taste. 2. Place a skillet on medium-high heat. Spray with cooking oil. Add the eggs. Scramble for 2 to 3 minutes, until the eggs are fluffy. Remove the eggs from the skillet and set aside. 3. If needed, spray the skillet with more oil. Add the chopped red and green bell peppers. Cook for 2 to 3 minutes, until the peppers are soft. 4. Add the sausage meat to the skillet. Break the sausage into smaller pieces using a spatula or spoon. Cook for 3 to 4 minutes, until the sausage is brown. 5. Add the salsa and scrambled eggs. Stir to combine. Remove the skillet from heat. 6. Spoon the mixture evenly onto the tortillas. 7. To form the burritos, fold the sides of each tortilla in toward the middle and then roll up from the bottom. You can secure each burrito with a toothpick. Or you can moisten the outside edge of the tortilla with a small amount of water. I prefer to use a cooking brush, but you can also dab with your fingers. 8. Spray the burritos with cooking oil and place them in the air fryer. Do not stack. Cook the burritos in batches if they do not all fit in the basket. Air fry at 204°C for 8 minutes. 9. Open the air fryer and flip the burritos. Cook for an additional 2 minutes or until crisp. 10. If necessary, repeat steps 8 and 9 for the remaining burritos. 11. Sprinkle the Cheddar cheese over the burritos. Cool before serving.

Bacon and Spinach Egg Muffins

Prep time: 7 minutes | Cook time: 12 to 14 minutes | Serves 6

6 large eggs	(optional)
60 ml double (whipping) cream	180 ml frozen chopped spinach,
½ teaspoon sea salt	thawed and drained
¼ teaspoon freshly ground	4 strips cooked bacon, crumbled
black pepper	60 g shredded Cheddar cheese
¼ teaspoon cayenne pepper	

1. In a large bowl (with a spout if you have one), whisk together the eggs, double cream, salt, black pepper, and cayenne pepper (if using). 2. Divide the spinach and bacon among 6 silicone muffin cups. Place the muffin cups in your air fryer basket. 3. Divide the egg mixture among the muffin cups. Top with the cheese. 4. Set the air fryer to 150°C. Bake for 12 to 14 minutes, until the eggs are set and cooked through.

Everything Bagels

Prep time: 15 minutes | Cook time: 14 minutes | Makes 6 bagels

415 ml shredded Mozzarella	vinegar
cheese or goat cheese	235 ml blanched almond flour
Mozzarella	1 tablespoon baking powder
2 tablespoons unsalted butter or	⅛ teaspoon fine sea salt
coconut oil	1½ teaspoons sesame seeds or
1 large egg, beaten	za'atar
1 tablespoon apple cider	

1. Make the dough: Put the Mozzarella and butter in a large microwave-safe bowl and microwave for 1 to 2 minutes, until the cheese is entirely melted. Stir well. Add the egg and vinegar. Using a hand mixer on medium, combine well. Add the almond flour, baking powder, and salt and, using the mixer, combine well. 2. Lay a piece of parchment paper on the countertop and place the dough on it. Knead it for about 3 minutes. The dough should be a little sticky but pliable. (If the dough is too sticky, chill it in the refrigerator for an hour or overnight.) 3. Preheat the air fryer to 176°C. Spray a baking sheet or pie pan that will fit into your air fryer with avocado oil. 4. Divide the dough into 6 equal portions. Roll 1 portion into a log that is 6 inches long and about ½ inch thick. Form the log into a circle and seal the edges together, making a bagel shape. Repeat with the remaining portions of dough, making 6 bagels. 5. Place the bagels on the greased baking sheet. Spray the bagels with avocado oil and top with everything bagel seasoning, pressing the seasoning into the dough with your hands. 6. Place the bagels in the air fryer and bake for 14 minutes, or until cooked through and golden brown, flipping after 6 minutes. 7. Remove the bagels from the air fryer and allow them to cool slightly before slicing them in half and serving. Store leftovers in an airtight container in the fridge for up to 4 days or in the freezer for up to a month.

Pancake Cake

Prep time: 10 minutes | Cook time: 7 minutes | Serves 4

120 ml blanched finely ground	softened
almond flour	1 large egg
60 ml powdered erythritol	½ teaspoon unflavoured gelatin
½ teaspoon baking powder	½ teaspoon vanilla extract
2 tablespoons unsalted butter,	½ teaspoon ground cinnamon

1. In a large bowl, mix almond flour, erythritol, and baking powder. Add butter, egg, gelatin, vanilla, and cinnamon. Pour into a round baking pan. 2. Place pan into the air fryer basket. 3. Adjust the temperature to 150°C and set the timer for 7 minutes. 4. When the cake is completely cooked, a toothpick will come out clean. Cut cake into four and serve.

Kale and Potato Nuggets

Prep time: 10 minutes | Cook time: 18 minutes | Serves 4

1 teaspoon extra virgin olive oil	30 ml milk
1 clove garlic, minced	Salt and ground black pepper,
1 L kale, rinsed and chopped	to taste
475 ml potatoes, boiled and	Cooking spray
mashed	

1. Preheat the air fryer to 200ºC. 2. In a skillet over medium heat, sauté the garlic in the olive oil, until it turns golden brown. Sauté with the kale for an additional 3 minutes and remove from the heat. 3. Mix the mashed potatoes, kale and garlic in a bowl. Pour in the milk and sprinkle with salt and pepper. 4. Shape the mixture into nuggets and spritz with cooking spray. 5. Put in the air fryer basket and air fry for 15 minutes, flip the nuggets halfway through cooking to make sure the nuggets fry evenly. 6. Serve immediately.

Tomato and Mozzarella Bruschetta

Prep time: 5 minutes | Cook time: 4 minutes | Serves 1

6 small loaf slices	1 tablespoon fresh basil,
120 ml tomatoes, finely	chopped
chopped	1 tablespoon olive oil
85 g Mozzarella cheese, grated	

1. Preheat the air fryer to 176ºC. 2. Put the loaf slices inside the air fryer and air fry for about 3 minutes. 3. Add the tomato, Mozzarella, basil, and olive oil on top. 4. Air fry for an additional minute before serving.

Homemade Cherry Breakfast Tarts

Prep time: 15 minutes | Cook time: 20 minutes | Serves 6

Tarts:	Frosting:
2 refrigerated piecrusts	120 ml vanilla yoghurt
80 ml cherry preserves	30 g cream cheese
1 teaspoon cornflour	1 teaspoon stevia
Cooking oil	Rainbow sprinkles

Make the Tarts 1. Place the piecrusts on a flat surface. Using a knife or pizza cutter, cut each piecrust into 3 rectangles, for 6 total. (I discard the unused dough left from slicing the edges.) 2. In a small bowl, combine the preserves and cornflour. Mix well. 3. Scoop 1 tablespoon of the preserves mixture onto the top half of each piece of piecrust. 4. Fold the bottom of each piece up to close the tart. Using the back of a fork, press along the edges of each tart to seal. 5. Spray the breakfast tarts with cooking oil and place them in the air fryer. I do not recommend stacking the breakfast tarts. They will stick together if stacked. You may need to prepare them in two batches. Bake at 375ºF for 10 minutes. 6. Allow the breakfast tarts

to cool fully before removing from the air fryer. 7. If necessary, repeat steps 5 and 6 for the remaining breakfast tarts. Make the Frosting 8. In a small bowl, combine the yoghurt, cream cheese, and stevia. Mix well. 9. Spread the breakfast tarts with frosting and top with sprinkles, and serve.

Poached Eggs on Whole Grain Avocado Toast

Prep time: 5 minutes | Cook time: 7 minutes | Serves 4

Olive oil cooking spray	4 pieces wholegrain bread
4 large eggs	1 avocado
Salt	Red pepper flakes (optional)
Black pepper	

1. Preheat the air fryer to 160ºC. Lightly coat the inside of four small oven-safe ramekins with olive oil cooking spray. 2. Crack one egg into each ramekin, and season with salt and black pepper. 3. Place the ramekins into the air fryer basket. Close and set the timer to 7 minutes. 4. While the eggs are cooking, toast the bread in a toaster. 5. Slice the avocado in half lengthwise, remove the pit, and scoop the flesh into a small bowl. Season with salt, black pepper, and red pepper flakes, if desired. Using a fork, smash the avocado lightly. 6. Spread a quarter of the smashed avocado evenly over each slice of toast. 7. Remove the eggs from the air fryer, and gently spoon one onto each slice of avocado toast before serving.

Nutty Granola

Prep time: 5 minutes | Cook time: 1 hour | Serves 4

120 ml pecans, coarsely	2 tablespoons sunflower seeds
chopped	2 tablespoons melted butter
120 ml walnuts or almonds,	60 ml granulated sweetener
coarsely chopped	½ teaspoon ground cinnamon
60 ml desiccated coconut	½ teaspoon vanilla extract
60 ml almond flour	¼ teaspoon ground nutmeg
60 ml ground flaxseed or chia	¼ teaspoon salt
seeds	2 tablespoons water

1. Preheat the air fryer to 120ºC. Cut a piece of parchment paper to fit inside the air fryer basket. 2. In a large bowl, toss the nuts, coconut, almond flour, ground flaxseed or chia seeds, sunflower seeds, butter, sweetener, cinnamon, vanilla, nutmeg, salt, and water until thoroughly combined. 3. Spread the granola on the parchment paper and flatten to an even thickness. 4. Air fry for about an hour, or until golden throughout. Remove from the air fryer and allow to fully cool. Break the granola into bite-size pieces and store in a covered container for up to a week.

Breakfast Cobbler

Prep time: 20 minutes | Cook time: 30 minutes | Serves 4

Filling:
280 g sausage meat, crumbled
60 ml minced onions
2 cloves garlic, minced
½ teaspoon fine sea salt
½ teaspoon ground black pepper
1 (230 g) package cream cheese (or cream cheese style spread for dairy-free), softened
180 ml beef or chicken stock
Biscuits:
3 large egg whites
180 ml blanched almond flour
1 teaspoon baking powder
¼ teaspoon fine sea salt
2½ tablespoons very cold unsalted butter, cut into ¼-inch pieces
Fresh thyme leaves, for garnish

1. Preheat the air fryer to 204ºC. 2. Place the sausage, onions, and garlic in a pie pan. Using your hands, break up the sausage into small pieces and spread it evenly throughout the pie pan. Season with the salt and pepper. Place the pan in the air fryer and bake for 5 minutes. 3. While the sausage cooks, place the cream cheese and stock in a food processor or blender and purée until smooth. 4. Remove the pork from the air fryer and use a fork or metal spatula to crumble it more. Pour the cream cheese mixture into the sausage and stir to combine. Set aside. 5. Make the biscuits: Place the egg whites in a medium-sized mixing bowl or the bowl of a stand mixer and whip with a hand mixer or stand mixer until stiff peaks form. 6. In a separate medium-sized bowl, whisk together the almond flour, baking powder, and salt, then cut in the butter. When you are done, the mixture should still have chunks of butter. Gently fold the flour mixture into the egg whites with a rubber spatula. 7. Use a large spoon or ice cream scoop to scoop the dough into 4 equal-sized biscuits, making sure the butter is evenly distributed. Place the biscuits on top of the sausage and cook in the air fryer for 5 minutes, then turn the heat down to 164ºC and bake for another 17 to 20 minutes, until the biscuits are golden brown. Serve garnished with fresh thyme leaves. 8. Store leftovers in an airtight container in the refrigerator for up to 3 days. Reheat in a preheated 176ºC air fryer for 5 minutes, or until warmed through.

Jalapeño Popper Egg Cups

Prep time: 10 minutes | Cook time: 10 minutes | Serves 2

4 large eggs
60 ml chopped pickled jalapeños
60 g full-fat cream cheese
120 ml shredded sharp Cheddar cheese

1. In a medium bowl, beat the eggs, then pour into four silicone muffin cups. 2. In a large microwave-safe bowl, place jalapeños, cream cheese, and Cheddar. Microwave for 30 seconds and stir. Take a spoonful, approximately ¼ of the mixture, and place it in the center of one of the egg cups. Repeat with remaining mixture. 3. Place egg cups into the air fryer basket. 4. Adjust the temperature to 160ºC and bake for 10 minutes. 5. Serve warm.

Simple Cinnamon Toasts

Prep time: 5 minutes | Cook time: 4 minutes | Serves 4

1 tablespoon salted butter
2 teaspoons ground cinnamon
4 tablespoons sugar
½ teaspoon vanilla extract
10 bread slices

1. Preheat the air fryer to 192ºC. 2. In a bowl, combine the butter, cinnamon, sugar, and vanilla extract. Spread onto the slices of bread. 3. Put the bread inside the air fryer and bake for 4 minutes or until golden brown. 4. Serve warm.

Easy Buttermilk Biscuits

Prep time: 5 minutes | Cook time: 18 minutes | Makes 16 biscuits

600 ml plain flour
1 tablespoon baking powder
1 teaspoon coarse or flaky salt
1 teaspoon sugar
½ teaspoon baking soda
8 tablespoons (1 stick) unsalted butter, at room temperature
235 ml buttermilk, chilled

1. Stir together the flour, baking powder, salt, sugar, and baking powder in a large bowl. 2. Add the butter and stir to mix well. Pour in the buttermilk and stir with a rubber spatula just until incorporated. 3. Place the dough onto a lightly floured surface and roll the dough out to a disk, ½ inch thick. Cut out the biscuits with a 2-inch round cutter and re-roll any scraps until you have 16 biscuits. 4. Preheat the air fryer to 164ºC. 5. Working in batches, arrange the biscuits in the air fryer basket in a single layer. Bake for about 18 minutes until the biscuits are golden brown. 6. Remove from the basket to a plate and repeat with the remaining biscuits. 7. Serve hot.

Egg in a Hole

Prep time: 5 minutes | Cook time: 5 minutes | Serves 1

1 slice bread
1 teaspoon butter, softened
1 egg
Salt and pepper, to taste
1 tablespoon shredded Cheddar cheese
2 teaspoons diced ham

1. Preheat the air fryer to 166ºC. Place a baking dish in the air fryer basket. 2. On a flat work surface, cut a hole in the center of the bread slice with a 2½-inch-diameter biscuit cutter. 3. Spread the butter evenly on each side of the bread slice and transfer to the baking dish. 4. Crack the egg into the hole and season as desired with salt and pepper. Scatter the shredded cheese and diced ham on top. 5. Bake in the preheated air fryer for 5 minutes until the bread is lightly browned and the egg is cooked to your preference. 6. Remove from the basket and serve hot.

Buffalo Chicken Breakfast Muffins

Prep time: 7 minutes | Cook time: 13 to 16 minutes | Serves 10

170 g shredded cooked chicken	1 teaspoon minced garlic
85 g blue cheese, crumbled	6 large eggs
2 tablespoons unsalted butter, melted	Sea salt and freshly ground black pepper, to taste
80 ml Buffalo hot sauce, such as Frank's RedHot	Avocado oil spray

1. In a large bowl, stir together the chicken, blue cheese, melted butter, hot sauce, and garlic. 2. In a medium bowl or large liquid measuring cup, beat the eggs. Season with salt and pepper. 3. Spray 10 silicone muffin cups with oil. Divide the chicken mixture among the cups, and pour the egg mixture over top. 4. Place the cups in the air fryer and set to 150ºC. Bake for 13 to 16 minutes, until the muffins are set and cooked through. (Depending on the size of your air fryer, you may need to cook the muffins in batches.)

Breakfast Sammies

Prep time: 15 minutes | Cook time: 20 minutes | Serves 5

Biscuits:	pieces
6 large egg whites	Eggs:
475 ml blanched almond flour, plus more if needed	5 large eggs
1½ teaspoons baking powder	½ teaspoon fine sea salt
½ teaspoon fine sea salt	¼ teaspoon ground black pepper
60 ml (½ stick) very cold unsalted butter (or lard for dairy-free), cut into ¼-inch	5 (30 g) slices Cheddar cheese (omit for dairy-free)
	10 thin slices ham

1. Spray the air fryer basket with avocado oil. Preheat the air fryer to 176ºC. Grease two pie pans or two baking pans that will fit inside your air fryer. 2. Make the biscuits: In a medium-sized bowl, whip the egg whites with a hand mixer until very stiff. Set aside. 3. In a separate medium-sized bowl, stir together the almond flour, baking powder, and salt until well combined. Cut in the butter. Gently fold the flour mixture into the egg whites with a rubber spatula. If the dough is too wet to form into mounds, add a few tablespoons of almond flour until the dough holds together well. 4. Using a large spoon, divide the dough into 5 equal portions and drop them about 1 inch apart on one of the greased pie pans. (If you're using a smaller air fryer, work in batches if necessary.) Place the pan in the air fryer and bake for 11 to 14 minutes, until the biscuits are golden brown. Remove from the air fryer and set aside to cool. 5. Make the eggs: Set the air fryer to 192ºC. Crack the eggs into the remaining greased pie pan and sprinkle with the salt and pepper. Place the eggs in the air fryer to bake for 5 minutes, or until they are cooked to your liking. 6. Open the air fryer and top each egg yolk with a slice of cheese (if using). Bake for another minute, or until the cheese is melted. 7. Once the biscuits are cool, slice them in half lengthwise. Place 1 cooked egg topped with cheese and 2 slices of ham in each biscuit. 8. Store leftover biscuits, eggs, and ham in separate airtight containers in the fridge for up to 3 days. Reheat the biscuits and eggs on a baking sheet in a preheated 176ºC air fryer for 5 minutes, or until warmed through.

White Bean–Oat Waffles

Prep time: 10 minutes | Cook time: 20 minutes | Serves 2

1 large egg white	drained and rinsed
2 tablespoons finely ground flaxseed	1 teaspoon coconut oil
120 ml water	1 teaspoon liquid sweetener
¼ teaspoon salt	120 ml old-fashioned rolled oats
1 teaspoon vanilla extract	Extra-virgin olive oil cooking spray
120 ml cannellini beans,	

1. In a blender, combine the egg white, flaxseed, water, salt, vanilla, cannellini beans, coconut oil, and sweetener. Blend on high for 90 seconds. 2. Add the oats. Blend for 1 minute more. 3. Preheat the waffle iron. The batter will thicken to the correct consistency while the waffle iron preheats. 4. Spray the heated waffle iron with cooking spray. 5. Add 180 ml batter. Close the waffle iron. Cook for 6 to 8 minutes, or until done. Repeated with the remaining batter. 6. Serve hot, with your favorite sugar-free topping.

Maple Granola

Prep time: 5 minutes | Cook time: 40 minutes | Makes 475 ml

235 ml rolled oats	sunflower
3 tablespoons pure maple syrup	¼ teaspoon sea salt
1 tablespoon sugar	¼ teaspoon ground cinnamon
1 tablespoon neutral-flavored oil, such as refined coconut or	¼ teaspoon vanilla extract

1. Insert the crisper plate into the basket and the basket into the unit. Preheat the unit by selecting BAKE, setting the temperature to 120ºC, and setting the time to 3 minutes. Select START/STOP to begin. 2. In a medium bowl, stir together the oats, maple syrup, sugar, oil, salt, cinnamon, and vanilla until thoroughly combined. Transfer the granola to a 6-by-2-inch round baking pan. 3. Once the unit is preheated, place the pan into the basket. 4. Select BAKE, set the temperature to 120ºC and set the time to 40 minutes. Select START/STOP to begin. 5. After 10 minutes, stir the granola well. Resume cooking, stirring the granola every 10 minutes, for a total of 40 minutes, or until the granola is lightly browned and mostly dry. 6. When the cooking is complete, place the granola on a plate to cool. It will become crisp as it cools. Store the completely cooled granola in an airtight container in a cool, dry place for 1 to 2 weeks.

Bacon, Egg, and Cheese Roll Ups

Prep time: 15 minutes | Cook time: 15 minutes | Serves 4

2 tablespoons unsalted butter	12 slices bacon
60 ml chopped onion	235 ml shredded sharp Cheddar
½ medium green pepper, seeded	cheese
and chopped	120 ml mild salsa, for dipping
6 large eggs	

1. In a medium skillet over medium heat, melt butter. Add onion and pepper to the skillet and sauté until fragrant and onions are translucent, about 3 minutes. 2. Whisk eggs in a small bowl and pour into skillet. Scramble eggs with onions and peppers until fluffy and fully cooked, about 5 minutes. Remove from heat and set aside. 3. On work surface, place three slices of bacon side by side, overlapping about ¼ inch. Place 60 ml scrambled eggs in a heap on the side closest to you and sprinkle 60 ml cheese on top of the eggs. 4. Tightly roll the bacon around the eggs and secure the seam with a toothpick if necessary. Place each roll into the air fryer basket. 5. Adjust the temperature to 176°C and air fry for 15 minutes. Rotate the rolls halfway through the cooking time. 6. Bacon will be brown and crispy when completely cooked. Serve immediately with salsa for dipping.

Bourbon Vanilla French Toast

Prep time: 15 minutes | Cook time: 6 minutes | Serves 4

2 large eggs	2 tablespoons bourbon
2 tablespoons water	1 teaspoon vanilla extract
160 ml whole or semi-skimmed	8 (1-inch-thick) French bread
milk	slices
1 tablespoon butter, melted	Cooking spray

1. Preheat the air fryer to 160°C. Line the air fryer basket with parchment paper and spray it with cooking spray. 2. Beat the eggs with the water in a shallow bowl until combined. Add the milk, melted butter, bourbon, and vanilla and stir to mix well. 3. Dredge 4 slices of bread in the batter, turning to coat both sides evenly. Transfer the bread slices onto the parchment paper. 4. Bake for 6 minutes until nicely browned. Flip the slices halfway through the cooking time. 5. Remove from the basket to a plate and repeat with the remaining 4 slices of bread. 6. Serve warm.

Breakfast Meatballs

Prep time: 10 minutes | Cook time: 15 minutes | Makes 18 meatballs

450 g pork sausage meat,	120 ml shredded sharp Cheddar
removed from casings	cheese
½ teaspoon salt	30 g cream cheese, softened
¼ teaspoon ground black	1 large egg, whisked
pepper	

1. Combine all ingredients in a large bowl. Form mixture into eighteen 1-inch meatballs. 2. Place meatballs into ungreased air fryer basket. Adjust the temperature to 204°C and air fry for 15 minutes, shaking basket three times during cooking. Meatballs will be browned on the outside and have an internal temperature of at least 64°C when completely cooked. Serve warm.

Onion Omelette

Prep time: 10 minutes | Cook time: 12 minutes | Serves 2

3 eggs	1 large onion, chopped
Salt and ground black pepper,	2 tablespoons grated Cheddar
to taste	cheese
½ teaspoons soy sauce	Cooking spray

1. Preheat the air fryer to 180°C. 2. In a bowl, whisk together the eggs, salt, pepper, and soy sauce. 3. Spritz a small pan with cooking spray. Spread the chopped onion across the bottom of the pan, then transfer the pan to the air fryer. 4. Bake in the preheated air fryer for 6 minutes or until the onion is translucent. 5. Add the egg mixture on top of the onions to coat well. Add the cheese on top, then continue baking for another 6 minutes. 6. Allow to cool before serving.

Chapter 2 Family Favorites

Chapter 2 Family Favorites

Chinese-Inspired Spareribs

Prep time: 30 minutes | Cook time: 8 minutes | Serves 4

Oil, for spraying	60 ml honey
340 g boneless pork spareribs,	2 tablespoons minced garlic
cut into 3-inch-long pieces	1 teaspoon ground ginger
235 ml soy sauce	2 drops red food colouring
180 ml sugar	(optional)
120 ml beef or chicken stock	

Line the air fryer basket with parchment and spray lightly with oil. Combine the ribs, soy sauce, sugar, beef stock, honey, garlic, ginger, and food colouring (if using) in a large zip-top plastic bag, seal, and shake well until completely coated. Refrigerate for at least 30 minutes. Place the ribs in the prepared basket. Air fry at 192°C for 8 minutes, or until the internal temperature reaches 74°C.

Cheesy Roasted Sweet Potatoes

Prep time: 7 minutes | Cook time: 18 to 23 minutes | Serves 4

2 large sweet potatoes, peeled	vinegar
and sliced	1 teaspoon dried thyme
1 teaspoon olive oil	60 ml grated Parmesan cheese
1 tablespoon white balsamic	

In a large bowl, drizzle the sweet potato slices with the olive oil and toss. Sprinkle with the balsamic vinegar and thyme and toss again. Sprinkle the potatoes with the Parmesan cheese and toss to coat. Roast the slices, in batches, in the air fryer basket at 204°C for 18 to 23 minutes, tossing the sweet potato slices in the basket once during cooking, until tender. Repeat with the remaining sweet potato slices. Serve immediately.

Bacon-Wrapped Hot Dogs

Prep time: 5 minutes | Cook time: 10 minutes | Serves 4

Oil, for spraying	4 hot dog buns
4 bacon slices	Toppings of choice
4 beef hot dogs	

Line the air fryer basket with parchment and spray lightly with oil. Wrap a strip of bacon tightly around each hot dog, taking care to cover the tips so they don't get too crispy. Secure with a toothpick at each end to keep the bacon from shrinking. Place the hot dogs in the prepared basket. Air fry at 192°C for 8 to 9 minutes, depending on how crispy you like the bacon. For extra-crispy, cook the hot dogs at 204°C for 6 to 8 minutes. Place the hot dogs in the buns, return them to the air fryer, and cook for another 1 to 2 minutes, or until the buns are warm. Add your desired toppings and serve.

Berry Cheesecake

Prep time: 5 minutes | Cook time: 10 minutes | Serves 4

Oil, for spraying	1 large egg
227 g soft white cheese	½ teaspoon vanilla extract
6 tablespoons sugar	¼ teaspoon lemon juice
1 tablespoon sour cream	120 ml fresh mixed berries

Preheat the air fryer to 176°C. Line the air fryer basket with parchment and spray lightly with oil. In a blender, combine the soft white cheese, sugar, sour cream, egg, vanilla, and lemon juice and blend until smooth. Pour the mixture into a 4-inch springform pan. Place the pan in the prepared basket. Cook for 8 to 10 minutes, or until only the very centre jiggles slightly when the pan is moved. Refrigerate the cheesecake in the pan for at least 2 hours. Release the sides from the springform pan, top the cheesecake with the mixed berries, and serve.

Steak Tips and Potatoes

Prep time: 10 minutes | Cook time: 20 minutes | Serves 4

Oil, for spraying	1 teaspoon Worcestershire
227 g baby gold potatoes, cut in	sauce
half	1 teaspoon granulated garlic
½ teaspoon salt	½ teaspoon salt
450 g steak, cut into ½-inch	½ teaspoon freshly ground
pieces	black pepper

Line the air fryer basket with parchment and spray lightly with oil. In a microwave-safe bowl, combine the potatoes and salt, then pour in about ½ inch of water. Microwave for 7 minutes, or until the potatoes are nearly tender. Drain. In a large bowl, gently mix together the steak, potatoes, Worcestershire sauce, garlic, salt, and black pepper. Spread the mixture in an even layer in the prepared basket. Air fry at 204°C for 12 to 17 minutes, stirring after 5 to 6 minutes. The cooking time will depend on the thickness of the meat and preferred doneness.

Pork Burgers with Red Cabbage Salad

Prep time: 20 minutes | Cook time: 7 to 9 minutes | Serves 4

120 ml Greek yoghurt	½ teaspoon paprika
2 tablespoons low-salt mustard, divided	235 ml mixed baby lettuce greens
1 tablespoon lemon juice	2 small tomatoes, sliced
60 ml sliced red cabbage	8 small low-salt wholemeal
60 ml grated carrots	sandwich buns, cut in half
450 g lean minced pork	

In a small bowl, combine the yoghurt, 1 tablespoon mustard, lemon juice, cabbage, and carrots; mix and refrigerate. In a medium bowl, combine the pork, remaining 1 tablespoon mustard, and paprika. Form into 8 small patties. Put the sliders into the air fryer basket. Air fry at 204ºC for 7 to 9 minutes, or until the sliders register 74ºC as tested with a meat thermometer. Assemble the burgers by placing some of the lettuce greens on a bun bottom. Top with a tomato slice, the burgers, and the cabbage mixture. Add the bun top and serve immediately.

Avocado and Egg Burrito

Prep time: 10 minutes | Cook time: 3 to 5 minutes | Serves 4

2 hard-boiled egg whites, chopped	plus additional for serving (optional)
1 hard-boiled egg, chopped	1 (34 g) slice low-salt, low-fat processed cheese, torn into pieces
1 avocado, peeled, pitted, and chopped	
1 red pepper, chopped	4 low-salt wholemeal flour tortillas
3 tablespoons low-salt salsa,	

In a medium bowl, thoroughly mix the egg whites, egg, avocado, red pepper, salsa, and cheese. Place the tortillas on a work surface and evenly divide the filling among them. Fold in the edges and roll up. Secure the burritos with toothpicks if necessary. Put the burritos in the air fryer basket. Air fry at 200ºC for 3 to 5 minutes, or until the burritos are light golden brown and crisp. Serve with more salsa (if using).

Meringue Cookies

Prep time: 15 minutes | Cook time: 1 hour 30 minutes | Makes 20 cookies

Oil, for spraying	235 ml sugar
4 large egg whites	Pinch cream of tartar

Preheat the air fryer to 60ºC. Line the air fryer basket with parchment and spray lightly with oil. In a small heatproof bowl, whisk together the egg whites and sugar. Fill a small saucepan halfway with water, place it over medium heat, and bring to a light simmer. Place the bowl with the egg whites on the saucepan, making sure the bottom of the bowl does not touch the water. Whisk the mixture until the sugar is dissolved. Transfer the mixture to a large bowl and add the cream of tartar. Using an electric mixer, beat the mixture on high until it is glossy and stiff peaks form. Transfer the mixture to a piping bag or a zip-top plastic bag with a corner cut off. Pipe rounds into the prepared basket. You may need to work in batches, depending on the size of your air fryer. Cook for 1 hour 30 minutes. Turn off the air fryer and let the meringues cool completely inside. The residual heat will continue to dry them out.

Old Bay Tilapia

Prep time: 15 minutes | Cook time: 6 minutes | Serves 4

Oil, for spraying	½ teaspoon salt
235 ml panko breadcrumbs	¼ teaspoon freshly ground black pepper
2 tablespoons Old Bay or all-purpose seasoning	1 large egg
2 teaspoons granulated garlic	4 tilapia fillets
1 teaspoon onion powder	

Preheat the air fryer to 204ºC. Line the air fryer basket with parchment and spray lightly with oil. In a shallow bowl, mix together the breadcrumbs, seasoning, garlic, onion powder, salt, and black pepper. In a small bowl, whisk the egg. Coat the tilapia in the egg, then dredge in the bread crumb mixture until completely coated. Place the tilapia in the prepared basket. You may need to work in batches, depending on the size of your air fryer. Spray lightly with oil. Cook for 4 to 6 minutes, depending on the thickness of the fillets, until the internal temperature reaches 64ºC. Serve immediately.

Fried Green Tomatoes

Prep time: 15 minutes | Cook time: 6 to 8 minutes | Serves 4

4 medium green tomatoes	120 ml panko breadcrumbs
80 ml plain flour	2 teaspoons olive oil
2 egg whites	1 teaspoon paprika
60 ml almond milk	1 clove garlic, minced
235 ml ground almonds	

Rinse the tomatoes and pat dry. Cut the tomatoes into ½-inch slices, discarding the thinner ends. Put the flour on a plate. In a shallow bowl, beat the egg whites with the almond milk until frothy. And on another plate, combine the almonds, breadcrumbs, olive oil, paprika, and garlic and mix well. Dip the tomato slices into the flour, then into the egg white mixture, then into the almond mixture to coat. Place four of the coated tomato slices in the air fryer basket. Air fry at 204ºC for 6 to 8 minutes or until the tomato coating is crisp and golden brown. Repeat with remaining tomato slices and serve immediately.

Chapter 3 Fast and Easy Everyday Favourites

Chapter 3 Fast and Easy Everyday Favourites

Easy Devils on Horseback

Prep time: 5 minutes | Cook time: 7 minutes | Serves 12

24 small pitted prunes (128 g)
60 ml crumbled blue cheese, divided

8 slices centre-cut bacon, cut crosswise into thirds

Preheat the air fryer to 204°C. Halve the prunes lengthwise, but don't cut them all the way through. Place ½ teaspoon of cheese in the centre of each prune. Wrap a piece of bacon around each prune and secure the bacon with a toothpick. Working in batches, arrange a single layer of the prunes in the air fryer basket. Air fry for about 7 minutes, flipping halfway, until the bacon is cooked through and crisp. Let cool slightly and serve warm.

Beery and Crunchy Onion Rings

Prep time: 10 minutes | Cook time: 16 minutes | Serves 2 to 4

160 ml plain flour
1 teaspoon paprika
½ teaspoon bicarbonate of soda
1 teaspoon salt
½ teaspoon freshly ground black pepper
1 egg, beaten

180 ml beer
350 ml breadcrumbs
1 tablespoons olive oil
1 large Vidalia or sweet onion, peeled and sliced into ½-inch rings
Cooking spray

Preheat the air fryer to 182°C. Spritz the air fryer basket with cooking spray. Combine the flour, paprika, bicarbonate of soda, salt, and ground black pepper in a bowl. Stir to mix well. Combine the egg and beer in a separate bowl. Stir to mix well. Make a well in the centre of the flour mixture, then pour the egg mixture in the well. Stir to mix everything well. Pour the breadcrumbs and olive oil in a shallow plate. Stir to mix well. Dredge the onion rings gently into the flour and egg mixture, then shake the excess off and put into the plate of breadcrumbs. Flip to coat both sides well. Arrange the onion rings in the preheated air fryer. Air fry in batches for 16 minutes or until golden brown and crunchy. Flip the rings and put the bottom rings to the top halfway through. Serve immediately.

Baked Halloumi with Greek Salsa

Prep timeBaked Halloumi with Greek Salsa

Salsa:
1 small shallot, finely diced
3 garlic cloves, minced
2 tablespoons fresh lemon juice
2 tablespoons extra-virgin olive oil
1 teaspoon freshly cracked black pepper
Pinch of rock salt
120 ml finely diced English cucumber
1 plum tomato, deseeded and

finely diced
2 teaspoons chopped fresh parsley
1 teaspoon snipped fresh dill
1 teaspoon snipped fresh oregano
Cheese:
227 g Halloumi cheese, sliced into ½-inch-thick pieces
1 tablespoon extra-virgin olive oil

Preheat the air fryer to 192°C. For the salsa: Combine the shallot, garlic, lemon juice, olive oil, pepper, and salt in a medium bowl. Add the cucumber, tomato, parsley, dill, and oregano. Toss gently to combine; set aside. For the cheese: Place the cheese slices in a medium bowl. Drizzle with the olive oil. Toss gently to coat. Arrange the cheese in a single layer in the air fryer basket. Bake for 6 minutes. Divide the cheese among four serving plates. Top with the salsa and serve immediately.

Buttery Sweet Potatoes

Prep time: 5 minutes | Cook time: 10 minutes | Serves 4

2 tablespoons butter, melted
1 tablespoon light brown sugar
2 sweet potatoes, peeled and cut

into ½-inch cubes
Cooking spray

Preheat the air fryer to 204°C. Line the air fryer basket with parchment paper. In a medium bowl, stir together the melted butter and brown sugar until blended. Toss the sweet potatoes in the butter mixture until coated. Place the sweet potatoes on the parchment and spritz with oil. Air fry for 5 minutes. Shake the basket, spritz the sweet potatoes with oil, and air fry for 5 minutes more until they're soft enough to cut with a fork. Serve immediately.

Simple Pea Delight

Prep time: 5 minutes | Cook time: 15 minutes | Serves 2 to 4

235 ml flour	3 tablespoons pea protein
1 teaspoon baking powder	120 ml chicken or turkey strips
3 eggs	Pinch of sea salt
235 ml coconut milk	235 ml Mozzarella cheese
235 ml soft white cheese	

Preheat the air fryer to 200°C. In a large bowl, mix all ingredients together using a large wooden spoon. Spoon equal amounts of the mixture into muffin cups and bake for 15 minutes. Serve immediately.

Cheesy Jalapeño Cornbread

Prep timeCheesy Jalapeño Cornbread

160 ml cornmeal	180 ml whole milk
80 ml plain flour	1 large egg, beaten
¾ teaspoon baking powder	1 jalapeño pepper, thinly sliced
2 tablespoons margarine, melted	80 ml shredded extra mature Cheddar cheese
½ teaspoon rock salt	Cooking spray
1 tablespoon granulated sugar	

Preheat the air fryer to 152°C. Spritz the air fryer basket with cooking spray. Combine all the ingredients in a large bowl. Stir to mix well. Pour the mixture in a baking pan. Arrange the pan in the preheated air fryer. Bake for 20 minutes or until a toothpick inserted in the centre of the bread comes out clean. When the cooking is complete, remove the baking pan from the air fryer and allow the bread to cool for a few minutes before slicing to serve.

Scalloped Veggie Mix

Prep time: 10 minutes | Cook time: 15 minutes | Serves 4

1 Yukon Gold or other small white potato, thinly sliced	60 ml minced onion
1 small sweet potato, peeled and thinly sliced	3 garlic cloves, minced
1 medium carrot, thinly sliced	180 ml 2 percent milk
	2 tablespoons cornflour
	½ teaspoon dried thyme

Preheat the air fryer to 192°C. In a baking pan, layer the potato, sweet potato, carrot, onion, and garlic. In a small bowl, whisk the milk, cornflour, and thyme until blended. Pour the milk mixture evenly over the vegetables in the pan. Bake for 15 minutes. Check the casserole—it should be golden brown on top, and the vegetables should be tender. Serve immediately.

Easy Roasted Asparagus

Prep time: 5 minutes | Cook time: 6 minutes | Serves 4

450 g asparagus, trimmed and halved crosswise	Salt and pepper, to taste
1 teaspoon extra-virgin olive oil	Lemon wedges, for serving

Preheat the air fryer to 204°C. Toss the asparagus with the oil, ⅛ teaspoon salt, and ⅛ teaspoon pepper in bowl. Transfer to air fryer basket. Place the basket in air fryer and roast for 6 to 8 minutes, or until tender and bright green, tossing halfway through cooking. Season with salt and pepper and serve with lemon wedges.

Cheesy Chilli Toast

Prep time: 5 minutes | Cook time: 5 minutes | Serves 1

2 tablespoons grated Parmesan cheese	room temperature
2 tablespoons grated Mozzarella cheese	10 to 15 thin slices serrano chilli or jalapeño
2 teaspoons salted butter, at	2 slices sourdough bread
	½ teaspoon black pepper

Preheat the air fryer to 164°C. In a small bowl, stir together the Parmesan, Mozzarella, butter, and chillies. Spread half the mixture onto one side of each slice of bread. Sprinkle with the pepper. Place the slices, cheese-side up, in the air fryer basket. Bake for 5 minutes, or until the cheese has melted and started to brown slightly. Serve immediately.

Baked Chorizo Scotch Eggs

Prep timeBaked Chorizo Scotch Eggs

450 g Mexican chorizo or other seasoned sausage meat

4 soft-boiled eggs plus 1 raw egg	120 ml plain flour
	235 ml panko breadcrumbs
1 tablespoon water	Cooking spray

Divide the chorizo into 4 equal portions. Flatten each portion into a disc. Place a soft-boiled egg in the centre of each disc. Wrap the chorizo around the egg, encasing it completely. Place the encased eggs on a plate and chill for at least 30 minutes. Preheat the air fryer to 182°C. Beat the raw egg with 1 tablespoon of water. Place the flour on a small plate and the panko on a second plate. Working with 1 egg at a time, roll the encased egg in the flour, then dip it in the egg mixture. Dredge the egg in the panko and place on a plate. Repeat with the remaining eggs. Spray the eggs with oil and place in the air fryer basket. Bake for 10 minutes. Turn and bake for an additional 5 to 10 minutes, or until browned and crisp on all sides. Serve immediately.

Beetroot Salad with Lemon Vinaigrette

Prep time: 10 minutes | Cook time: 12 to 15 minutes | Serves 4

6 medium red and golden beetroots, peeled and sliced	Cooking spray
1 teaspoon olive oil	Vinaigrette:
¼ teaspoon rock salt	2 teaspoons olive oil
120 ml crumbled feta cheese	2 tablespoons chopped fresh chives
2 L mixed greens	Juice of 1 lemon

Preheat the air fryer to 182ºC. In a large bowl, toss the beetroots, olive oil, and rock salt. Spray the air fryer basket with cooking spray, then place the beetroots in the basket and air fry for 12 to 15 minutes or until tender. While the beetroots cook, make the vinaigrette in a large bowl by whisking together the olive oil, lemon juice, and chives. Remove the beetroots from the air fryer, toss in the vinaigrette, and allow to cool for 5 minutes. Add the feta and serve on top of the mixed greens.

Herb-Roasted Veggies

Prep time: 10 minutes | Cook time: 14 to 18 minutes | Serves 4

1 red pepper, sliced	80 ml diced red onion
1 (230 g) package sliced mushrooms	3 garlic cloves, sliced
235 ml green beans, cut into 2-inch pieces	1 teaspoon olive oil
	½ teaspoon dried basil
	½ teaspoon dried tarragon

Preheat the air fryer to 176ºC. In a medium bowl, mix the red pepper, mushrooms, green beans, red onion, and garlic. Drizzle with the olive oil. Toss to coat. Add the herbs and toss again. Place the vegetables in the air fryer basket. Roast for 14 to 18 minutes, or until tender. Serve immediately.

Air Fried Butternut Squash with Chopped Hazelnuts

Prep time: 10 minutes | Cook time: 20 minutes | Makes 700 ml

2 tablespoons whole hazelnuts	¼ teaspoon freshly ground black pepper
700 ml butternut squash, peeled, deseeded, and cubed	2 teaspoons olive oil
¼ teaspoon rock salt	Cooking spray

Preheat the air fryer to 152ºC. Spritz the air fryer basket with cooking spray. Arrange the hazelnuts in the preheated air fryer. Air fry for 3 minutes or until soft. Chopped the hazelnuts roughly and transfer to a small bowl. Set aside. Set the air fryer temperature to 182ºC. Spritz with cooking spray. Put the butternut squash in a large bowl, then sprinkle with salt and pepper and drizzle with olive oil. Toss to coat well. Transfer the squash in the air fryer. Air fry for 20 minutes or until the squash is soft. Shake the basket halfway through the frying time. When the frying is complete, transfer the squash onto a plate and sprinkle with chopped hazelnuts before serving.

Bacon Pinwheels

Prep time: 10 minutes | Cook time: 10 minutes | Makes 8 pinwheels

1 sheet puff pastry	8 slices bacon
2 tablespoons maple syrup	Ground black pepper, to taste
60 ml brown sugar	Cooking spray

Preheat the air fryer to 182ºC. Spritz the air fryer basket with cooking spray. Roll the puff pastry into a 10-inch square with a rolling pin on a clean work surface, then cut the pastry into 8 strips. Brush the strips with maple syrup and sprinkle with sugar, leaving a 1-inch far end uncovered. Arrange each slice of bacon on each strip, leaving a ⅛-inch length of bacon hang over the end close to you. Sprinkle with black pepper. From the end close to you, roll the strips into pinwheels, then dab the uncovered end with water and seal the rolls. Arrange the pinwheels in the preheated air fryer and spritz with cooking spray. Air fry for 10 minutes or until golden brown. Flip the pinwheels halfway through. Serve immediately.

Cheesy Potato Patties

Prep time: 5 minutes | Cook time: 10 minutes | Serves 8

900 g white potatoes	½ teaspoon hot paprika
120 ml finely chopped spring onions	475 ml shredded Colby or Monterey Jack cheese
½ teaspoon freshly ground black pepper, or more to taste	60 ml rapeseed oil
1 tablespoon fine sea salt	235 ml crushed crackers

Preheat the air fryer to 182ºC. Boil the potatoes until soft. Dry them off and peel them before mashing thoroughly, leaving no lumps. Combine the mashed potatoes with spring onions, pepper, salt, paprika, and cheese. Mould the mixture into balls with your hands and press with your palm to flatten them into patties. In a shallow dish, combine the rapeseed oil and crushed crackers. Coat the patties in the crumb mixture. Bake the patties for about 10 minutes, in multiple batches if necessary. Serve hot.

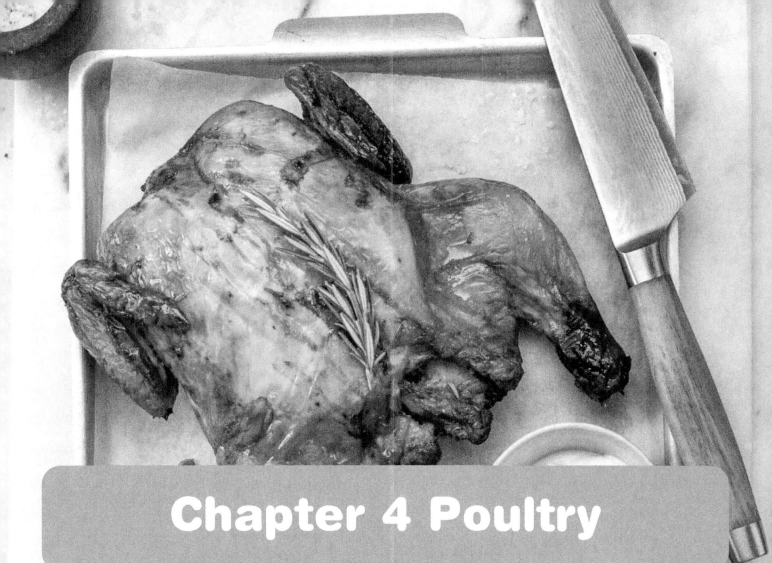

Chapter 4 Poultry

Chapter 4 Poultry

Barbecue Chicken Bites

Prep time: 5 minutes | Cook time: 19 minutes | Serves 4

Oil, for spraying
2 (170 g) boneless, skinless chicken breasts, cut into bite-size pieces
60 g all-purpose flour
1 tablespoon granulated garlic
2 teaspoons seasoned salt
280 g barbecue sauce

1. Line the air fryer basket with parchment and spray lightly with oil. 2. Place the chicken, flour, garlic, and seasoned salt in a zip-top plastic bag, seal, and shake well until evenly coated. 3. Place the chicken in an even layer in the prepared basket and spray liberally with oil. You may need to work in batches, depending on the size of your air fryer. 4. Roast at 200ºC for 8 minutes, flip, spray with more oil, and cook for another 8 minutes, or until the internal temperature reaches 76ºC and the juices run clear. 5. Transfer the chicken to a large bowl and toss with the barbecue sauce. 6. Line the air fryer basket with fresh parchment, return the chicken to the basket, and cook for another 3 minutes.

Gochujang Chicken Wings

Prep time: 15 minutes | Cook time: 25 minutes | Serves 4

Wings:
900 g chicken wings
1 teaspoon kosher salt
1 teaspoon black pepper or gochugaru (Korean red pepper)
Sauce:
2 tablespoons gochujang (Korean chili paste)
1 tablespoon mayonnaise
1 tablespoon toasted sesame oil
1 tablespoon minced fresh ginger
1 tablespoon minced garlic
1 teaspoon sugar
1 teaspoon agave nectar or honey
For Serving
1 teaspoon sesame seeds
25 g chopped spring onions

1. For the wings: Season the wings with the salt and pepper and place in the air fryer basket. Set the air fryer to 200ºC for 20 minutes, turning the wings halfway through the cooking time. 2. Meanwhile, for the sauce: In a small bowl, combine the gochujang, mayonnaise, sesame oil, ginger, garlic, sugar, and agave; set aside. 3. As you near the 20-minute mark, use a meat thermometer to check the meat. When the wings reach 70ºC, transfer them to a large bowl. Pour about half the sauce on the wings; toss to coat (serve the remaining sauce as a dip). 4. Return the wings to the air fryer basket and cook for 5 minutes, until the sauce has glazed. 5.

Transfer the wings to a serving platter. Sprinkle with the sesame seeds and spring onions. Serve with the reserved sauce on the side for dipping.

Blackened Chicken

Prep time: 10 minutes | Cook time: 20 minutes | Serves 4

1 large egg, beaten
215 g Blackened seasoning
2 whole boneless, skinless
chicken breasts (about 450 g each), halved
1 to 2 tablespoons oil

1. Place the beaten egg in one shallow bowl and the Blackened seasoning in another shallow bowl. 2. One at a time, dip the chicken pieces in the beaten egg and the Blackened seasoning, coating thoroughly. 3. Preheat the air fryer to 180ºC. Line the air fryer basket with parchment paper. 4. Place the chicken pieces on the parchment and spritz with oil. 5. Cook for 10 minutes. Flip the chicken, spritz it with oil, and cook for 10 minutes more until the internal temperature reaches 76ºC and the chicken is no longer pink inside. Let sit for 5 minutes before serving.

Cranberry Curry Chicken

Prep time: 12 minutes | Cook time: 18 minutes | Serves 4

3 (140 g) low-sodium boneless, skinless chicken breasts, cut into 1½-inch cubes
2 teaspoons olive oil
2 tablespoons cornflour
1 tablespoon curry powder
1 tart apple, chopped
120 ml low-sodium chicken broth
60 g dried cranberries
2 tablespoons freshly squeezed orange juice
Brown rice, cooked (optional)

1. Preheat the air fryer to 196ºC. 2. In a medium bowl, mix the chicken and olive oil. Sprinkle with the cornflour and curry powder. Toss to coat. Stir in the apple and transfer to a metal pan. Bake in the air fryer for 8 minutes, stirring once during cooking. 3. Add the chicken broth, cranberries, and orange juice. Bake for about 10 minutes more, or until the sauce is slightly thickened and the chicken reaches an internal temperature of 76ºC on a meat thermometer. Serve over hot cooked brown rice, if desired.

Barbecued Chicken with Creamy Coleslaw

Prep time: 10 minutes | Cook time: 20 minutes | Serves 2

270 g shredded coleslaw mix	plus extra for serving
Salt and pepper	2 tablespoons mayonnaise
2 (340 g) bone-in split chicken	2 tablespoons sour cream
breasts, trimmed	1 teaspoon distilled white
1 teaspoon vegetable oil	vinegar, plus extra for seasoning
2 tablespoons barbecue sauce,	¼ teaspoon sugar

1. Preheat the air fryer to 180ºC. 2. Toss coleslaw mix and ¼ teaspoon salt in a colander set over bowl. Let sit until wilted slightly, about 30 minutes. Rinse, drain, and dry well with a dish towel. 3. Meanwhile, pat chicken dry with paper towels, rub with oil, and season with salt and pepper. Arrange breasts skin-side down in air fryer basket, spaced evenly apart, alternating ends. Bake for 10 minutes. Flip breasts and brush skin side with barbecue sauce. Return basket to air fryer and bake until well browned and chicken registers 70ºC, 10 to 15 minutes. 4. Transfer chicken to serving platter, tent loosely with aluminum foil, and let rest for 5 minutes. While chicken rests, whisk mayonnaise, sour cream, vinegar, sugar, and pinch pepper together in a large bowl. Stir in coleslaw mix and season with salt, pepper, and additional vinegar to taste. Serve chicken with coleslaw, passing extra barbecue sauce separately.

Bacon-Wrapped Chicken Breasts Rolls

Prep time: 10 minutes | Cook time: 15 minutes | Serves 4

15 g chopped fresh chives	½ teaspoon red pepper flakes
2 tablespoons lemon juice	4 (115 g) boneless, skinless
1 teaspoon dried sage	chicken breasts, pounded to ¼
1 teaspoon fresh rosemary	inch thick
leaves	8 slices bacon
15 g fresh parsley leaves	Sprigs of fresh rosemary, for
4 cloves garlic, peeled	garnish
1 teaspoon ground fennel	Cooking spray
3 teaspoons sea salt	

1. Preheat the air fryer to 170ºC. Spritz the air fryer basket with cooking spray. 2. Put the chives, lemon juice, sage, rosemary, parsley, garlic, fennel, salt, and red pepper flakes in a food processor, then pulse to purée until smooth. 3. Unfold the chicken breasts on a clean work surface, then brush the top side of the chicken breasts with the sauce. 4. Roll the chicken breasts up from the shorter side, then wrap each chicken rolls with 2 bacon slices to cover. Secure with toothpicks. 5. Arrange the rolls in the preheated air fryer, then cook for 10 minutes. Flip the rolls halfway through. 6. Increase the heat to 200ºC and air fry for 5 more minutes or until the bacon is browned and crispy. 7. Transfer the rolls to a large plate. Discard the toothpicks and spread with rosemary sprigs before serving.

Buttermilk-Fried Drumsticks

Prep time: 10 minutes | Cook time: 25 minutes | Serves 2

1 egg	1 teaspoon salt
120 g buttermilk	¼ teaspoon ground black
90 g self-rising flour	pepper (to mix into coating)
90 g seasoned panko bread	4 chicken drumsticks, skin on
crumbs	Oil for misting or cooking spray

1. Beat together egg and buttermilk in shallow dish. 2. In a second shallow dish, combine the flour, panko crumbs, salt, and pepper. 3. Sprinkle chicken legs with additional salt and pepper to taste. 4. Dip legs in buttermilk mixture, then roll in panko mixture, pressing in crumbs to make coating stick. Mist with oil or cooking spray. 5. Spray the air fryer basket with cooking spray. 6. Cook drumsticks at 180ºC for 10 minutes. Turn pieces over and cook an additional 10 minutes. 7. Turn pieces to check for browning. If you have any white spots that haven't begun to brown, spritz them with oil or cooking spray. Continue cooking for 5 more minutes or until crust is golden brown and juices run clear. Larger, meatier drumsticks will take longer to cook than small ones.

Piri-Piri Chicken Thighs

Prep time: 5 minutes | Cook time: 25 minutes | Serves 4

60 ml piri-piri sauce	1 tablespoon extra-virgin olive
1 tablespoon freshly squeezed	oil
lemon juice	4 bone-in, skin-on chicken
2 tablespoons brown sugar,	thighs, each weighing
divided	approximately 200 to 230 g
2 cloves garlic, minced	½ teaspoon cornflour

1. To make the marinade, whisk together the piri-piri sauce, lemon juice, 1 tablespoon of brown sugar, and the garlic in a small bowl. While whisking, slowly pour in the oil in a steady stream and continue to whisk until emulsified. Using a skewer, poke holes in the chicken thighs and place them in a small glass dish. Pour the marinade over the chicken and turn the thighs to coat them with the sauce. Cover the dish and refrigerate for at least 15 minutes and up to 1 hour. 2. Preheat the air fryer to 190ºC. Remove the chicken thighs from the dish, reserving the marinade, and place them skin-side down in the air fryer basket. Air fry until the internal temperature reaches 76ºC, 15 to 20 minutes. 3. Meanwhile, whisk the remaining brown sugar and the cornflour into the marinade and microwave it on high power for 1 minute until it is bubbling and thickened to a glaze. 4. Once the chicken is cooked, turn the thighs over and brush them with the glaze. Air fry for a few additional minutes until the glaze browns and begins to char in spots. 5. Remove the chicken to a platter and serve with additional piri-piri sauce, if desired.

Golden Tenders

Prep time: 10 minutes | Cook time: 15 minutes | Serves 4

120 g panko bread crumbs	black pepper
1 tablespoon paprika	16 chicken tenders
½ teaspoon salt	115 g mayonnaise
¼ teaspoon freshly ground	Olive oil spray

1. In a medium bowl, stir together the panko, paprika, salt, and pepper. 2. In a large bowl, toss together the chicken tenders and mayonnaise to coat. Transfer the coated chicken pieces to the bowl of seasoned panko and dredge to coat thoroughly. Press the coating onto the chicken with your fingers. 3. Insert the crisper plate into the basket and the basket into the unit. Preheat the unit by selecting AIR FRY, setting the temperature to 180°C, and setting the time to 3 minutes. Select START/STOP to begin. 4. Once the unit is preheated, place a parchment paper liner into the basket. Place the chicken into the basket and spray it with olive oil. 5. Select AIR FRY, set the temperature to 180°C, and set the time to 15 minutes. Select START/STOP to begin. 6. When the cooking is complete, the tenders will be golden brown and a food thermometer inserted into the chicken should register 76°C. For more even browning, remove the basket halfway through cooking and flip the tenders. Give them an extra spray of olive oil and reinsert the basket to resume cooking. This ensures they are crispy and brown all over. 7. When the cooking is complete, serve.

Spinach and Feta Stuffed Chicken Breasts

Prep time: 10 minutes | Cook time: 27 minutes | Serves 4

1 (280 g) package frozen spinach, thawed and drained well	black pepper
	4 boneless chicken breasts
80 g feta cheese, crumbled	Salt and freshly ground black pepper, to taste
½ teaspoon freshly ground	1 tablespoon olive oil

1. Prepare the filling. Squeeze out as much liquid as possible from the thawed spinach. Rough chop the spinach and transfer it to a mixing bowl with the feta cheese and the freshly ground black pepper. 2. Prepare the chicken breast. Place the chicken breast on a cutting board and press down on the chicken breast with one hand to keep it stabilized. Make an incision about 1-inch long in the fattest side of the breast. Move the knife up and down inside the chicken breast, without poking through either the top or the bottom, or the other side of the breast. The inside pocket should be about 3-inches long, but the opening should only be about 1-inch wide. If this is too difficult, you can make the incision longer, but you will have to be more careful when cooking the chicken breast since this will expose more of the stuffing. 3. Once you have prepared the chicken breasts, use your fingers to stuff the filling into each pocket, spreading the mixture down as far as you can. 4. Preheat the air fryer to 190°C. 5. Lightly brush or spray the air fryer basket and the chicken breasts with olive oil. Transfer two of the stuffed chicken breasts to the air fryer. Air fry for 12 minutes, turning the chicken breasts over halfway through the cooking time. Remove the chicken to a resting plate and air fry the second two breasts for 12 minutes. Return the first batch of chicken to the air fryer with the second batch and air fry for 3 more minutes. When the chicken is cooked, an instant read thermometer should register 76°C in the thickest part of the chicken, as well as in the stuffing. 6. Remove the chicken breasts and let them rest on a cutting board for 2 to 3 minutes. Slice the chicken on the bias and serve with the slices fanned out.

Garlic Soy Chicken Thighs

Prep time: 10 minutes | Cook time: 30 minutes | Serves 1 to 2

2 tablespoons chicken stock	2 large spring onions, cut into 2- to 3-inch batons, plus more, thinly sliced, for garnish
2 tablespoons reduced-sodium soy sauce	
1½ tablespoons sugar	2 bone-in, skin-on chicken thighs (198 to 225 g each)
4 garlic cloves, smashed and peeled	

1. Preheat the air fryer to 190°C. 2. In a metal cake pan, combine the chicken stock, soy sauce, and sugar and stir until the sugar dissolves. Add the garlic cloves, spring onions, and chicken thighs, turning the thighs to coat them in the marinade, then resting them skin-side up. Place the pan in the air fryer and bake, flipping the thighs every 5 minutes after the first 10 minutes, until the chicken is cooked through and the marinade is reduced to a sticky glaze over the chicken, about 30 minutes. 3. Remove the pan from the air fryer and serve the chicken thighs warm, with any remaining glaze spooned over top and sprinkled with more sliced spring onions.

Italian Chicken Thighs

Prep time: 5 minutes | Cook time: 20 minutes | Serves 2

4 bone-in, skin-on chicken thighs	1 teaspoon dried basil
	½ teaspoon garlic powder
2 tablespoons unsalted butter, melted	¼ teaspoon onion powder
	¼ teaspoon dried oregano
1 teaspoon dried parsley	

1. Brush chicken thighs with butter and sprinkle remaining ingredients over thighs. Place thighs into the air fryer basket. 2. Adjust the temperature to 190°C and roast for 20 minutes. 3. Halfway through the cooking time, flip the thighs. 4. When fully cooked, internal temperature will be at least 76°C and skin will be crispy. Serve warm.

Simply Terrific Turkey Meatballs

Prep time: 10 minutes | Cook time: 7 to 10 minutes | Serves 4

1 red bell pepper, seeded and coarsely chopped	1 egg, lightly beaten
2 cloves garlic, coarsely chopped	45 g grated Parmesan cheese
15 g chopped fresh parsley	1 teaspoon salt
680 g 85% lean turkey mince	½ teaspoon freshly ground black pepper

1. Preheat the air fryer to 200°C. 2. In a food processor fitted with a metal blade, combine the bell pepper, garlic, and parsley. Pulse until finely chopped. Transfer the vegetables to a large mixing bowl. 3. Add the turkey, egg, Parmesan, salt, and black pepper. Mix gently until thoroughly combined. Shape the mixture into 1¼-inch meatballs. 4. Working in batches if necessary, arrange the meatballs in a single layer in the air fryer basket; coat lightly with olive oil spray. Pausing halfway through the cooking time to shake the basket, air fry for 7 to 10 minutes, until lightly browned and a thermometer inserted into the centre of a meatball registers 76°C.

Chicken Rochambeau

Prep time: 15 minutes | Cook time: 20 minutes | Serves 4

1 tablespoon butter	Sauce:
4 chicken tenders, cut in half crosswise	2 tablespoons butter
Salt and pepper, to taste	25 g chopped green onions
30 g flour	50 g chopped mushrooms
Oil for misting	2 tablespoons flour
4 slices ham, ¼- to ⅜-inches thick and large enough to cover an English muffin	240 ml chicken broth
	¼ teaspoon garlic powder
2 English muffins, split	1½ teaspoons Worcestershire sauce

1. Place 1 tablespoon of butter in a baking pan and air fry at 200°C for 2 minutes to melt. 2. Sprinkle chicken tenders with salt and pepper to taste, then roll in the flour. 3. Place chicken in baking pan, turning pieces to coat with melted butter. 4. Air fry at 200°C for 5 minutes. Turn chicken pieces over, and spray tops lightly with olive oil. Cook 5 minutes longer or until juices run clear. The chicken will not brown. 5. While chicken is cooking, make the sauce: In a medium saucepan, melt the 2 tablespoons of butter. 6. Add onions and mushrooms and sauté until tender, about 3 minutes. 7. Stir in the flour. Gradually add broth, stirring constantly until you have a smooth gravy. 8. Add garlic powder and Worcestershire sauce and simmer on low heat until sauce thickens, about 5 minutes. 9. When chicken is cooked, remove baking pan from air fryer and set aside. 10. Place ham slices directly into air fryer basket and air fry at 200°C for 5 minutes or until hot and beginning to sizzle a little.

Remove and set aside on top of the chicken for now. 11. Place the English muffin halves in air fryer basket and air fry at 200°C for 1 minute. 12. Open air fryer and place a ham slice on top of each English muffin half. Stack 2 pieces of chicken on top of each ham slice. Air fry for 1 to 2 minutes to heat through. 13. Place each English muffin stack on a serving plate and top with plenty of sauce.

Chicken Hand Pies

Prep time: 30 minutes | Cook time: 10 minutes per batch | Makes 8 pies

180 ml chicken broth	1 tablespoon milk
130 g frozen mixed peas and carrots	Salt and pepper, to taste
140 g cooked chicken, chopped	1 (8-count) can organic flaky biscuits
1 tablespoon cornflour	Oil for misting or cooking spray

1. In a medium saucepan, bring chicken broth to a boil. Stir in the frozen peas and carrots and cook for 5 minutes over medium heat. Stir in chicken. 2. Mix the cornflour into the milk until it dissolves. Stir it into the simmering chicken broth mixture and cook just until thickened. 3. Remove from heat, add salt and pepper to taste, and let cool slightly. 4. Lay biscuits out on wax paper. Peel each biscuit apart in the middle to make 2 rounds so you have 16 rounds total. Using your hands or a rolling pin, flatten each biscuit round slightly to make it larger and thinner. 5. Divide chicken filling among 8 of the biscuit rounds. Place remaining biscuit rounds on top and press edges all around. Use the tines of a fork to crimp biscuit edges and make sure they are sealed well. 6. Spray both sides lightly with oil or cooking spray. 7. Cook in a single layer, 4 at a time, at 170°C for 10 minutes or until biscuit dough is cooked through and golden brown.

Tex-Mex Chicken Breasts

Prep time: 10 minutes | Cook time: 17 to 20 minutes | Serves 4

450 g low-sodium boneless, skinless chicken breasts, cut into 1-inch cubes	2 teaspoons olive oil
1 medium onion, chopped	115 g canned low-sodium black beans, rinsed and drained
1 red bell pepper, chopped	130 g low-sodium salsa
1 jalapeño pepper, minced	2 teaspoons chili powder

1. Preheat the air fryer to 200°C. 2. In a medium metal bowl, mix the chicken, onion, bell pepper, jalapeño, and olive oil. Roast for 10 minutes, stirring once during cooking. 3. Add the black beans, salsa, and chili powder. Roast for 7 to 10 minutes more, stirring once, until the chicken reaches an internal temperature of 76°C on a meat thermometer. Serve immediately.

Ranch Chicken Wings

Prep time: 10 minutes | Cook time: 40 minutes | Serves 4

2 tablespoons water	1 (30 g) envelope ranch salad
2 tablespoons hot pepper sauce	dressing mix
2 tablespoons unsalted butter,	1 teaspoon paprika
melted	4 1.8 kg chicken wings, tips
2 tablespoons apple cider	removed
vinegar	Cooking oil spray

1. In a large bowl, whisk the water, hot pepper sauce, melted butter, vinegar, salad dressing mix, and paprika until combined. 2. Add the wings and toss to coat. At this point, you can cover the bowl and marinate the wings in the refrigerator for 4 to 24 hours for best results. However, you can just let the wings stand for 30 minutes in the refrigerator. 3. Insert the crisper plate into the basket and the basket into the unit. Preheat the unit by selecting AIR FRY, setting the temperature to 200ºC, and setting the time to 3 minutes. Select START/STOP to begin. 4. Once the unit is preheated, spray the crisper plate with cooking oil. Working in batches, put half the wings into the basket; it is okay to stack them. Refrigerate the remaining wings. 5. Select AIR FRY, set the temperature to 200ºC, and set the time to 20 minutes. Select START/STOP to begin. 6. After 5 minutes, remove the basket and shake it. Reinsert the basket to resume cooking. Remove and shake the basket every 5 minutes, three more times, until the chicken is browned and glazed and a food thermometer inserted into the wings registers 76ºC. 7. Repeat steps 4, 5, and 6 with the remaining wings. 8. When the cooking is complete, serve warm.

Wild Rice and Kale Stuffed Chicken Thighs

Prep time: 10 minutes | Cook time: 22 minutes | Serves 4

4 boneless, skinless chicken	1 teaspoon salt
thighs	Juice of 1 lemon
250 g cooked wild rice	100 g crumbled feta
35 g chopped kale	Olive oil cooking spray
2 garlic cloves, minced	1 tablespoon olive oi

1. Preheat the air fryer to 192ºC. 2. Place the chicken thighs between two pieces of plastic wrap, and using a meat mallet or a rolling pin, pound them out to about ¼-inch thick. 3. In a medium bowl, combine the rice, kale, garlic, salt, and lemon juice and mix well. 4. Place a quarter of the rice mixture into the middle of each chicken thigh, then sprinkle 2 tablespoons of feta over the filling. 5. Spray the air fryer basket with olive oil cooking spray. 6. Fold the sides of the chicken thigh over the filling, and then gently place each of them seam-side down into the air fryer basket. Brush each stuffed chicken thigh with olive oil. 7. Roast the stuffed chicken thighs for 12 minutes, then turn them over and cook for an additional 10 minutes, or until the internal temperature reaches 76ºC.

Butter and Bacon Chicken

Prep time: 10 minutes | Cook time: 65 minutes | Serves 6

1 (1.8 kg) whole chicken	1 teaspoon salt
2 tablespoons salted butter,	½ teaspoon ground black
softened	pepper
1 teaspoon dried thyme	6 slices sugar-free bacon
½ teaspoon garlic powder	

1. Pat chicken dry with a paper towel, then rub with butter on all sides. Sprinkle thyme, garlic powder, salt, and pepper over chicken. 2. Place chicken into ungreased air fryer basket, breast side up. Lay strips of bacon over chicken and secure with toothpicks. 3. Adjust the temperature to 180ºC and air fry for 65 minutes. Halfway through cooking, remove and set aside bacon and flip chicken over. Chicken will be done when the skin is golden and crispy and the internal temperature is at least 76ºC. Serve warm with bacon.

Greek Chicken Stir-Fry

Prep time: 15 minutes | Cook time: 15 minutes | Serves 2

1 (170 g) chicken breast, cut	and sliced
into 1-inch cubes	1 tablespoon coconut oil
½ medium courgette, chopped	1 teaspoon dried oregano
½ medium red bell pepper,	½ teaspoon garlic powder
seeded and chopped	¼ teaspoon dried thyme
¼ medium red onion, peeled	

1. Place all ingredients into a large mixing bowl and toss until the coconut oil coats the meat and vegetables. Pour the contents of the bowl into the air fryer basket. 2. Adjust the temperature to (190ºC and air fry for 15 minutes. 3. Shake the basket halfway through the cooking time to redistribute the food. Serve immediately.

Almond-Crusted Chicken

Prep time: 15 minutes | Cook time: 25 minutes | Serves 4

20 g slivered almonds	2 tablespoons full-fat
2 (170 g) boneless, skinless	mayonnaise
chicken breasts	1 tablespoon Dijon mustard

1. Pulse the almonds in a food processor or chop until finely chopped. Place almonds evenly on a plate and set aside. 2. Completely slice each chicken breast in half lengthwise. 3. Mix the mayonnaise and mustard in a small bowl and then coat chicken with the mixture. 4. Lay each piece of chicken in the chopped almonds to fully coat. Carefully move the pieces into the air fryer basket. 5. Adjust the temperature to 180ºC and air fry for 25 minutes. 6. Chicken will be done when it has reached an internal temperature of 76ºC or more. Serve warm.

Italian Flavour Chicken Breasts with Roma Tomatoes

Prep time: 10 minutes | Cook time: 60 minutes | Serves 8

1.4 kg chicken breasts, bone-in	½ teaspoon salt
1 teaspoon minced fresh basil	½ teaspoon freshly ground
1 teaspoon minced fresh	black pepper
rosemary	4 medium Roma tomatoes,
2 tablespoons minced fresh	halved
parsley	Cooking spray
1 teaspoon cayenne pepper	

1. Preheat the air fryer to 190ºC. Spritz the air fryer basket with cooking spray. 2. Combine all the ingredients, except for the chicken breasts and tomatoes, in a large bowl. Stir to mix well. 3. Dunk the chicken breasts in the mixture and press to coat well. 4. Transfer the chicken breasts in the preheated air fryer. You may need to work in batches to avoid overcrowding. 5. Air fry for 25 minutes or until the internal temperature of the thickest part of the breasts reaches at least 76ºC. Flip the breasts halfway through the cooking time. 6. Remove the cooked chicken breasts from the basket and adjust the temperature to 180ºC. 7. Place the tomatoes in the air fryer and spritz with cooking spray. Sprinkle with a touch of salt and cook for 10 minutes or until tender. Shake the basket halfway through the cooking time. 8. Serve the tomatoes with chicken breasts on a large serving plate.

Smoky Chicken Leg Quarters

Prep time: 30 minutes | Cook time: 23 to 27 minutes | Serves 6

120 ml avocado oil	½ teaspoon dried thyme
2 teaspoons smoked paprika	½ teaspoon freshly ground
1 teaspoon sea salt	black pepper
1 teaspoon garlic powder	900 g bone-in, skin-on chicken
½ teaspoon dried rosemary	leg quarters

1. In a blender or small bowl, combine the avocado oil, smoked paprika, salt, garlic powder, rosemary, thyme, and black pepper. 2. Place the chicken in a shallow dish or large zip-top bag. Pour the marinade over the chicken, making sure all the legs are coated. Cover and marinate for at least 2 hours or overnight. 3. Place the chicken in a single layer in the air fryer basket, working in batches if necessary. Set the air fryer to 200ºC and air fry for 15 minutes. Flip the chicken legs, then reduce the temperature to 180ºC. . Cook for 8 to 12 minutes more, until an instant-read thermometer reads 70ºC when inserted into the thickest piece of chicken. 4. Allow to rest for 5 to 10 minutes before serving.

Easy Chicken Nachos

Prep time: 5 minutes | Cook time: 5 minutes | Serves 8

Oil, for spraying	55 g corn tortilla chips
420 g shredded cooked chicken	75 g bacon bits
1 (30 g) package ranch	235 g shredded Cheddar cheese
seasoning	1 tablespoon chopped spring
60 g sour cream	onions

1. Line the air fryer basket with parchment and spray lightly with oil. 2. In a small bowl, mix together the chicken, ranch seasoning, and sour cream. 3. Place the tortilla chips in the prepared basket and top with the chicken mixture. Add the bacon bits, Cheddar cheese, and spring onions. 4. Air fry at 220ºC for 3 to 5 minutes, or until heated through and the cheese is melted.

Curried Orange Honey Chicken

Prep time: 10 minutes | Cook time: 16 to 19 minutes | Serves 4

340 g boneless, skinless chicken	60 ml chicken stock
thighs, cut into 1-inch pieces	2 tablespoons honey
1 yellow bell pepper, cut into	60 ml orange juice
1½-inch pieces	1 tablespoon cornflour
1 small red onion, sliced	2 to 3 teaspoons curry powder
Olive oil for misting	

1. Preheat the air fryer to 190ºC. 2. Put the chicken thighs, pepper, and red onion in the air fryer basket and mist with olive oil. 3. Roast for 12 to 14 minutes or until the chicken is cooked to 76ºC, shaking the basket halfway through cooking time. 4. Remove the chicken and vegetables from the air fryer basket and set aside. 5. In a metal bowl, combine the stock, honey, orange juice, cornflour, and curry powder, and mix well. Add the chicken and vegetables, stir, and put the bowl in the basket. 6. Return the basket to the air fryer and roast for 2 minutes. Remove and stir, then roast for 2 to 3 minutes or until the sauce is thickened and bubbly. 7. Serve warm.

Chapter 5 Beef, Pork, and Lamb

Chapter 5 Beef, Pork, and Lamb

Sausage and Peppers

Prep time: 7 minutes | Cook time: 35 minutes | Serves 4

Oil, for spraying	1 tablespoon olive oil
900 g hot or sweet Italian-	1 tablespoon chopped fresh
seasoned sausage links, cut into	parsley
thick slices	1 teaspoon dried oregano
4 large peppers of any color,	1 teaspoon dried basil
seeded and cut into slices	1 teaspoon balsamic vinegar
1 onion, thinly sliced	

1. Line the air fryer basket with parchment and spray lightly with oil. 2. In a large bowl, combine the sausage, peppers, and onion. 3. In a small bowl, whisk together the olive oil, parsley, oregano, basil, and balsamic vinegar. Pour the mixture over the sausage and peppers and toss until evenly coated. 4. Using a slotted spoon, transfer the mixture to the prepared basket, taking care to drain out as much excess liquid as possible. 5. Air fry at 176°C for 20 minutes, stir, and cook for another 15 minutes, or until the sausage is browned and the juices run clear.

Sausage and Cauliflower Arancini

Prep time: 30 minutes | Cook time: 28 to 32 minutes | Serves 6

Avocado oil spray	85 g cream cheese
170 g Italian-seasoned sausage,	110 g Cheddar cheese, shredded
casings removed	1 large egg
60 ml diced onion	120 ml finely ground blanched
1 teaspoon minced garlic	almond flour
1 teaspoon dried thyme	60 ml finely grated Parmesan
Sea salt and freshly ground	cheese
black pepper, to taste	Keto-friendly marinara sauce,
120 ml cauliflower rice	for serving

1. Spray a large skillet with oil and place it over medium-high heat. Once the skillet is hot, put the sausage in the skillet and cook for 7 minutes, breaking up the meat with the back of a spoon. 2. Reduce the heat to medium and add the onion. Cook for 5 minutes, then add the garlic, thyme, and salt and pepper to taste. Cook for 1 minute more. 3. Add the cauliflower rice and cream cheese to the skillet. Cook for 7 minutes, stirring frequently, until the cream cheese melts and the cauliflower is tender. 4. Remove the skillet from the heat and stir in the Cheddar cheese. Using a cookie scoop,

form the mixture into 1½-inch balls. Place the balls on a parchment paper-lined baking sheet. Freeze for 30 minutes. 5. Place the egg in a shallow bowl and beat it with a fork. In a separate bowl, stir together the almond flour and Parmesan cheese. 6. Dip the cauliflower balls into the egg, then coat them with the almond flour mixture, gently pressing the mixture to the balls to adhere. 7. Set the air fryer to 204°C. Spray the cauliflower rice balls with oil, and arrange them in a single layer in the air fryer basket, working in batches if necessary. Air fry for 5 minutes. Flip the rice balls and spray them with more oil. Air fry for 3 to 7 minutes longer, until the balls are golden brown. 8. Serve warm with marinara sauce.

Chinese-Style Baby Back Ribs

Prep time: 30 minutes | Cook time: 30 minutes | Serves 4

1 tablespoon toasted sesame oil	1 tablespoon agave nectar or
1 tablespoon fermented black	honey
bean paste	1 teaspoon minced garlic
1 tablespoon Shaoxing wine	1 teaspoon minced fresh ginger
(rice cooking wine)	1 (680 g) slab baby back ribs,
1 tablespoon dark soy sauce	cut into individual ribs

1. In a large bowl, stir together the sesame oil, black bean paste, wine, soy sauce, agave, garlic, and ginger. Add the ribs and toss well to coat. Marinate at room temperature for 30 minutes, or cover and refrigerate for up to 24 hours. 2. Place the ribs in the air fryer basket; discard the marinade. Set the air fryer to 176°C for 30 minutes.

Baby Back Ribs

Prep time: 5 minutes | Cook time: 25 minutes | Serves 4

900 g baby back ribs	¼ teaspoon ground cayenne
2 teaspoons chili powder	pepper
1 teaspoon paprika	120 ml low-carb, sugar-free
½ teaspoon onion granules	barbecue sauce
½ teaspoon garlic powder	

1. Rub ribs with all ingredients except barbecue sauce. Place into the air fryer basket. 2. Adjust the temperature to 204°C and roast for 25 minutes. 3. When done, ribs will be dark and charred with an internal temperature of at least 85°C. Brush ribs with barbecue sauce and serve warm.

German Rouladen-Style Steak

Prep time: 20 minutes | Cook time: 15 minutes | Serves 4

Onion Sauce:	parsley
2 medium onions, cut into	Rouladen:
½-inch-thick slices	60 ml Dijon mustard
Coarse or flaky salt and black	450 g bavette or skirt steak, ¼
pepper, to taste	to ½ inch thick
120 ml sour cream	1 teaspoon black pepper
1 tablespoon tomato paste	4 slices bacon
2 teaspoons chopped fresh	60 ml chopped fresh parsley

1. For the sauce: In a small bowl, mix together the onions with salt and pepper to taste. Place the onions in the air fryer basket. Set the air fryer to 204°C for 6 minutes, or until the onions are softened and golden brown. 2. Set aside half of the onions to use in the rouladen. Place the rest in a small bowl and add the sour cream, tomato paste, parsley, ½ teaspoon salt, and ½ teaspoon pepper. Stir until well combined, adding 1 to 2 tablespoons of water, if necessary, to thin the sauce slightly. Set the sauce aside. 3. For the rouladen: Evenly spread the mustard over the meat. Sprinkle with the pepper. Top with the bacon slices, reserved onions, and parsley. Starting at the long end, roll up the steak as tightly as possible, ending seam side down. Use 2 or 3 wooden toothpicks to hold the roll together. Using a sharp knife, cut the roll in half so that it better fits in the air fryer basket. 4. Place the steak, seam side down, in the air fryer basket. Set the air fryer to 204°C for 9 minutes. Use a meat thermometer to ensure the steak has reached an internal temperature of 64°C. (It is critical to not overcook bavette steak, so as to not toughen the meat.) 5. Let the steak rest for 10 minutes before cutting into slices. Serve with the sauce.

Spinach and Mozzarella Steak Rolls

Prep time: 10 minutes | Cook time: 12 minutes |
Makes 8 rolls

1 (450 g) bavette or skirt steak, butterflied	235 ml fresh spinach leaves
8 (30 g, ¼-inch-thick) slices low-moisture Mozzarella or other melting cheese	½ teaspoon salt
	¼ teaspoon ground black pepper

1. Place steak on a large plate. Place Mozzarella slices to cover steak, leaving 1-inch at the edges. Lay spinach leaves over cheese. Gently roll steak and tie with kitchen twine or secure with toothpicks. Carefully slice into eight pieces. Sprinkle each with salt and pepper. 2. Place rolls into ungreased air fryer basket, cut side up. Adjust the temperature to 204°C and air fry for 12 minutes. Steak rolls will be browned and cheese will be melted when done and have an internal temperature of at least 64°C for medium steak and 82°C for well-done steak. Serve warm.

Cantonese BBQ Pork

Prep time: 30 minutes | Cook time: 15 minutes | Serves 4

60 ml honey	2 teaspoons minced garlic
2 tablespoons dark soy sauce	2 teaspoons minced fresh ginger
1 tablespoon sugar	1 teaspoon Chinese five-spice
1 tablespoon Shaoxing wine (rice cooking wine)	powder
1 tablespoon hoisin sauce	450 g fatty pork shoulder, cut into long, 1-inch-thick pieces

1. In a small microwave-safe bowl, combine the honey, soy sauce, sugar, wine, hoisin, garlic, ginger, and five-spice powder. Microwave in 10-second intervals, stirring in between, until the honey has dissolved. 2. Use a fork to pierce the pork slices to allow the marinade to penetrate better. Place the pork in a large bowl or resealable plastic bag and pour in half the marinade; set aside the remaining marinade to use for the sauce. Toss to coat. Marinate the pork at room temperature for 30 minutes, or cover and refrigerate for up 24 hours. 3. Place the pork in a single layer in the air fryer basket. Set the air fryer to 204°C for 15 minutes, turning and basting the pork halfway through the cooking time. 4. While the pork is cooking, microwave the reserved marinade on high for 45 to 60 seconds, stirring every 15 seconds, to thicken it slightly to the consistency of a sauce. 5. Transfer the pork to a cutting board and let rest for 10 minutes. Brush with the sauce and serve.

Mojito Lamb Chops

Prep time: 30 minutes | Cook time: 5 minutes | Serves 2

Marinade:	2 teaspoons fine sea salt
2 teaspoons grated lime zest	½ teaspoon ground black
120 ml lime juice	pepper
60 ml avocado oil	4 (1-inch-thick) lamb chops
60 ml chopped fresh mint leaves	Sprigs of fresh mint, for garnish (optional)
4 cloves garlic, roughly chopped	Lime slices, for serving (optional)

1. Make the marinade: Place all the ingredients for the marinade in a food processor or blender and purée until mostly smooth with a few small chunks. Transfer half of the marinade to a shallow dish and set the other half aside for serving. Add the lamb to the shallow dish, cover, and place in the refrigerator to marinate for at least 2 hours or overnight. 2. Spray the air fryer basket with avocado oil. Preheat the air fryer to 200°C. 3. Remove the chops from the marinade and place them in the air fryer basket. Air fry for 5 minutes, or until the internal temperature reaches 64°C for medium doneness. 4. Allow the chops to rest for 10 minutes before serving with the rest of the marinade as a sauce. Garnish with fresh mint leaves and serve with lime slices, if desired. Best served fresh.

Parmesan-Crusted Pork Chops

Prep time: 5 minutes | Cook time: 12 minutes | Serves 4

1 large egg	½ teaspoon salt
120 ml grated Parmesan cheese	¼ teaspoon ground black
4 (110 g) boneless pork chops	pepper

1. Whisk egg in a medium bowl and place Parmesan in a separate medium bowl. 2. Sprinkle pork chops on both sides with salt and pepper. Dip each pork chop into egg, then press both sides into Parmesan. 3. Place pork chops into ungreased air fryer basket. Adjust the temperature to 204ºC and air fry for 12 minutes, turning chops halfway through cooking. Pork chops will be golden and have an internal temperature of at least 64ºC when done. Serve warm.

Pork Schnitzel with Dill Sauce

Prep time: 5 minutes | Cook time: 24 minutes |
Serves 4 to 6

6 bonelesspork chops (about 680 g)	3 tablespoons butter, melted
120 ml flour	2 tablespoons vegetable or olive oil
1½ teaspoons salt	lemon wedges
Freshly ground black pepper, to taste	Dill Sauce:
2 eggs	235 ml chicken stock
120 ml milk	1½ tablespoons cornflour
355 ml toasted fine bread crumbs	80 ml sour cream
1 teaspoon paprika	1½ tablespoons chopped fresh dill
	Salt and pepper, to taste

1. Trim the excess fat from the pork chops and pound each chop with a meat mallet between two pieces of plastic wrap until they are ½-inch thick. 2. Set up a dredging station. Combine the flour, salt, and black pepper in a shallow dish. Whisk the eggs and milk together in a second shallow dish. Finally, combine the bread crumbs and paprika in a third shallow dish. 3. Dip each flattened pork chop in the flour. Shake off the excess flour and dip each chop into the egg mixture. Finally dip them into the bread crumbs and press the bread crumbs onto the meat firmly. Place each finished chop on a baking sheet until they are all coated. 4. Preheat the air fryer to 204ºC. 5. Combine the melted butter and the oil in a small bowl and lightly brush both sides of the coated pork chops. Do not brush the chops too heavily or the breading will not be as crispy. 6. Air fry one schnitzel at a time for 4 minutes, turning it over halfway through the cooking time. Hold the cooked schnitzels warm on a baking pan in a 76ºC oven while you finish air frying the rest. 7. While the schnitzels are cooking, whisk the chicken stock and cornflour together in a small saucepan over medium-high heat on the stovetop. Bring the mixture to a boil and simmer for 2 minutes.

Remove the saucepan from heat and whisk in the sour cream. Add the chopped fresh dill and season with salt and pepper. 8. Transfer the pork schnitzel to a platter and serve with dill sauce and lemon wedges.

Pork Shoulder with Garlicky Coriander-Parsley Sauce

Prep time: 1 hour 15 minutes | Cook time: 30 minutes | Serves 4

1 teaspoon flaxseed meal	to taste
1 egg white, well whisked	Garlicky Coriander-Parsley
1 tablespoon soy sauce	Sauce:
1 teaspoon lemon juice, preferably freshly squeezed	3 garlic cloves, minced
	80 ml fresh coriander leaves
1 tablespoon olive oil	80 ml fresh parsley leaves
450 g pork shoulder, cut into pieces 2-inches long	1 teaspoon lemon juice
	½ tablespoon salt
Salt and ground black pepper,	80 ml extra-virgin olive oil

1. Combine the flaxseed meal, egg white, soy sauce, lemon juice, salt, black pepper, and olive oil in a large bowl. Dunk the pork strips in and press to submerge. 2. Wrap the bowl in plastic and refrigerate to marinate for at least an hour. 3. Preheat the air fryer to 192ºC. 4. Arrange the marinated pork strips in the preheated air fryer and air fry for 30 minutes or until cooked through and well browned. Flip the strips halfway through. 5. Meanwhile, combine the ingredients for the sauce in a small bowl. Stir to mix well. Arrange the bowl in the refrigerator to chill until ready to serve. 6. Serve the air fried pork strips with the chilled sauce.

Bone-in Pork Chops

Prep time: 5 minutes | Cook time: 10 to 12 minutes |
Serves 2

450 g bone-in pork chops	¼ teaspoon cayenne pepper
1 tablespoon avocado oil	Sea salt and freshly ground
1 teaspoon smoked paprika	black pepper, to taste
½ teaspoon onion granules	

1. Brush the pork chops with the avocado oil. In a small dish, mix together the smoked paprika, onion granules, cayenne pepper, and salt and black pepper to taste. Sprinkle the seasonings over both sides of the pork chops. 2. Set the air fryer to 204ºC. Place the chops in the air fryer basket in a single layer, working in batches if necessary. Air fry for 10 to 12 minutes, until an instant-read thermometer reads 64ºC at the chops' thickest point. 3. Remove the chops from the air fryer and allow them to rest for 5 minutes before serving.

Fillet with Crispy Shallots

Prep time: 30 minutes | Cook time: 18 to 20 minutes | Serves 6

680 g beef fillet steaks	4 medium shallots
Sea salt and freshly ground black pepper, to taste	1 teaspoon olive oil or avocado oil

1. Season both sides of the steaks with salt and pepper, and let them sit at room temperature for 45 minutes. 2. Set the air fryer to 204°C and let it preheat for 5 minutes. 3. Working in batches if necessary, place the steaks in the air fryer basket in a single layer and air fry for 5 minutes. Flip and cook for 5 minutes longer, until an instant-read thermometer inserted in the center of the steaks registers 49°C for medium-rare (or as desired). Remove the steaks and tent with aluminum foil to rest. 4. Set the air fryer to 149°C. In a medium bowl, toss the shallots with the oil. Place the shallots in the basket and air fry for 5 minutes, then give them a toss and cook for 3 to 5 minutes more, until crispy and golden brown. 5. Place the steaks on serving plates and arrange the shallots on top.

Lamb Burger with Feta and Olives

Prep time: 10 minutes | Cook time: 20 minutes | Serves 3 to 4

2 teaspoons olive oil	120 ml black olives, finely chopped
⅓ onion, finely chopped	80 ml crumbled feta cheese
1 clove garlic, minced	½ teaspoon salt
450 g lamb mince	Freshly ground black pepper, to taste
2 tablespoons fresh parsley, finely chopped	4 thick pitta breads
1½ teaspoons fresh oregano, finely chopped	

1. Preheat a medium skillet over medium-high heat on the stovetop. Add the olive oil and cook the onion until tender, but not browned, about 4 to 5 minutes. Add the garlic and cook for another minute. Transfer the onion and garlic to a mixing bowl and add the lamb mince, parsley, oregano, olives, feta cheese, salt and pepper. Gently mix the ingredients together. 2. Divide the mixture into 3 or 4 equal portions and then form the hamburgers, being careful not to over-handle the meat. One good way to do this is to throw the meat back and forth between your hands like a baseball, packing the meat each time you catch it. Flatten the balls into patties, making an indentation in the center of each patty. Flatten the sides of the patties as well to make it easier to fit them into the air fryer basket. 3. Preheat the air fryer to 188°C. 4. If you don't have room for all four burgers, air fry two or three burgers at a time for 8 minutes at 188°C. Flip the burgers over and air fry for another 8 minutes. If you cooked your burgers in batches, return the first batch of burgers to the air fryer for the last two minutes of cooking to re-heat. This should give you a medium-well burger. If you'd prefer a medium-rare burger, shorten the cooking time to about 13 minutes. Remove the burgers to a resting plate and let the burgers rest for a few minutes before dressing and serving. 5. While the burgers are resting, toast the pitta breads in the air fryer for 2 minutes. Tuck the burgers into the toasted pitta breads, or wrap the pittas around the burgers and serve with a tzatziki sauce or some mayonnaise.

Mediterranean Beef Steaks

Prep time: 20 minutes | Cook time: 20 minutes | Serves 4

2 tablespoons soy sauce or tamari	pepper
	½ teaspoon dried basil
3 heaping tablespoons fresh chives	½ teaspoon dried rosemary
	1 teaspoon freshly ground black pepper
2 tablespoons olive oil	
3 tablespoons dry white wine	1 teaspoon sea salt, or more to taste
4 small-sized beef steaks	
2 teaspoons smoked cayenne	

1. Firstly, coat the steaks with the cayenne pepper, black pepper, salt, basil, and rosemary. 2. Drizzle the steaks with olive oil, white wine, and soy sauce. 3. Finally, roast in the air fryer for 20 minutes at 172°C. Serve garnished with fresh chives. Bon appétit!

Roast Beef with Horseradish Cream

Prep time: 5 minutes | Cook time: 35 to 45 minutes | Serves 6

900 g beef roasting joint	80 ml double cream
1 tablespoon salt	80 ml sour cream
2 teaspoons garlic powder	80 ml grated horseradish
1 teaspoon freshly ground black pepper	2 teaspoons fresh lemon juice
	Salt and freshly ground black pepper, to taste
1 teaspoon dried thyme	
Horseradish Cream:	

1. Preheat the air fryer to 204°C. 2. Season the beef with the salt, garlic powder, black pepper, and thyme. Place the beef fat-side down in the basket of the air fryer and lightly coat with olive oil. Pausing halfway through the cooking time to turn the meat, air fry for 35 to 45 minutes, until a thermometer inserted into the thickest part indicates the desired doneness, 52°C (rare) to 64°C (medium). Let the beef rest for 10 minutes before slicing. 3. To make the horseradish cream: In a small bowl, combine the double cream, sour cream, horseradish, and lemon juice. Whisk until thoroughly combined. Season to taste with salt and freshly ground black pepper. Serve alongside the beef.

Vietnamese Grilled Pork

Prep time: 30 minutes | Cook time: 20 minutes | Serves 6

60 ml minced brown onion	½ teaspoon black pepper
2 tablespoons sugar	680 g boneless pork shoulder,
2 tablespoons vegetable oil	cut into ½-inch-thick slices
1 tablespoon minced garlic	60 ml chopped salted roasted
1 tablespoon fish sauce	peanuts
1 tablespoon minced fresh	2 tablespoons chopped fresh
lemongrass	coriander or parsley
2 teaspoons dark soy sauce	

1. In a large bowl, combine the onion, sugar, vegetable oil, garlic, fish sauce, lemongrass, soy sauce, and pepper. Add the pork and toss to coat. Marinate at room temperature for 30 minutes, or cover and refrigerate for up to 24 hours. 2. Arrange the pork slices in the air fryer basket; discard the marinade. Set the air fryer to 204°C for 20 minutes, turning the pork halfway through the cooking time. 3. Transfer the pork to a serving platter. Sprinkle with the peanuts and coriander and serve.

Ritzy Skirt Steak Fajitas

Prep time: 15 minutes | Cook time: 30 minutes | Serves 4

2 tablespoons olive oil	1 green pepper, sliced
60 ml lime juice	Salt and freshly ground black
1 clove garlic, minced	pepper, to taste
½ teaspoon ground cumin	8 flour tortillas
½ teaspoon hot sauce	Toppings:
½ teaspoon salt	Shredded lettuce
2 tablespoons chopped fresh	Crumbled feta or ricotta (or
coriander	grated Cheddar cheese)
450 g skirt steak	Sliced black olives
1 onion, sliced	Diced tomatoes
1 teaspoon chili powder	Sour cream
1 red pepper, sliced	Guacamole

1. Combine the olive oil, lime juice, garlic, cumin, hot sauce, salt and coriander in a shallow dish. Add the skirt steak and turn it over several times to coat all sides. Pierce the steak with a needle-style meat tenderizer or paring knife. Marinate the steak in the refrigerator for at least 3 hours, or overnight. When you are ready to cook, remove the steak from the refrigerator and let it sit at room temperature for 30 minutes. 2. Preheat the air fryer to 204°C. 3. Toss the onion slices with the chili powder and a little olive oil and transfer them to the air fryer basket. Air fry for 5 minutes. Add the red and green peppers to the air fryer basket with the onions, season with salt and pepper and air fry for 8 more minutes, until the onions and peppers are soft. Transfer the vegetables to a dish and cover with aluminum foil to keep warm. 4. Put the skirt steak in the air fryer basket and pour the marinade over the top. Air fry at 204°C for 12 minutes. Flip the steak over and air fry for an additional 5 minutes. Transfer the cooked steak to a cutting board and let the steak rest for a few minutes. If the peppers and onions need to be heated, return them to the air fryer for just 1 to 2 minutes. 5. Thinly slice the steak at an angle, cutting against the grain of the steak. Serve the steak with the onions and peppers, the warm tortillas and the fajita toppings on the side.

Green Pepper Cheeseburgers

Prep time: 5 minutes | Cook time: 30 minutes | Serves 4

2 green peppers	black pepper
680 g 85% lean beef mince	4 slices Cheddar cheese (about
1 clove garlic, minced	85 g)
1 teaspoon salt	4 large lettuce leaves
½ teaspoon freshly ground	

1. Preheat the air fryer to 204°C. 2. Arrange the peppers in the basket of the air fryer. Pausing halfway through the cooking time to turn the peppers, air fry for 20 minutes, or until they are softened and beginning to char. Transfer the peppers to a large bowl and cover with a plate. When cool enough to handle, peel off the skin, remove the seeds and stems, and slice into strips. Set aside. 3. Meanwhile, in a large bowl, combine the beef with the garlic, salt, and pepper. Shape the beef into 4 patties. 4. Lower the heat on the air fryer to 182°C. Arrange the burgers in a single layer in the basket of the air fryer. Pausing halfway through the cooking time to turn the burgers, air fry for 10 minutes, or until a thermometer inserted into the thickest part registers 72°C. 5. Top the burgers with the cheese slices and continue baking for a minute or two, just until the cheese has melted. Serve the burgers on a lettuce leaf topped with the roasted peppers.

Italian Pork Loin

Prep time: 30 minutes | Cook time: 16 minutes | Serves 3

1 teaspoon sea salt	2 garlic cloves, minced
½ teaspoon black pepper,	450 g pork loin joint
freshly cracked	1 tablespoon Italian herb
60 ml red wine	seasoning blend
2 tablespoons mustard	

1. In a ceramic bowl, mix the salt, black pepper, red wine, mustard, and garlic. Add the pork loin and let it marinate at least 30 minutes. 2. Spritz the sides and bottom of the air fryer basket with nonstick cooking spray. 3. Place the pork loin in the basket; sprinkle with the Italian herb seasoning blend. Cook the pork loin at 188°C for 10 minutes. Flip halfway through, spraying with cooking oil and cook for 5 to 6 minutes more. Serve immediately.

Bacon and Cheese Stuffed Pork Chops

Prep time: 10 minutes | Cook time: 12 minutes | Serves 4

15 g plain pork scratchings, finely crushed	crumbled
120 ml shredded sharp Cheddar cheese	4 (110 g) boneless pork chops
	½ teaspoon salt
4 slices cooked bacon,	¼ teaspoon ground black pepper

1. In a small bowl, mix pork scratchings, Cheddar, and bacon. 2. Make a 3-inch slit in the side of each pork chop and stuff with ¼ pork rind mixture. Sprinkle each side of pork chops with salt and pepper. 3. Place pork chops into ungreased air fryer basket, stuffed side up. Adjust the temperature to 204°C and air fry for 12 minutes. Pork chops will be browned and have an internal temperature of at least 64°C when done. Serve warm.

Chuck Kebab with Rocket

Prep time: 30 minutes | Cook time: 25 minutes | Serves 4

120 ml leeks, chopped	½ teaspoon ground sumac
2 garlic cloves, smashed	3 saffron threads
900 g beef mince	2 tablespoons loosely packed fresh flat-leaf parsley leaves
Salt, to taste	
¼ teaspoon ground black pepper, or more to taste	4 tablespoons tahini sauce
	110 g baby rocket
1 teaspoon cayenne pepper	1 tomato, cut into slices

1. In a bowl, mix the chopped leeks, garlic, beef mince, and spices; knead with your hands until everything is well incorporated. 2. Now, mound the beef mixture around a wooden skewer into a pointed-ended sausage. 3. Cook in the preheated air fryer at 182°C for 25 minutes. Serve your kebab with the tahini sauce, baby rocket and tomato. Enjoy!

Broccoli and Pork Teriyaki

Prep time: 10 minutes | Cook time: 13 minutes | Serves 4

1 head broccoli, trimmed into florets	450 g pork tenderloin, trimmed and cut into 1-inch pieces
1 tablespoon extra-virgin olive oil	120 ml teriyaki sauce, divided
	Olive oil spray
¼ teaspoon sea salt	475 ml cooked brown rice
¼ teaspoon freshly ground black pepper	Sesame seeds, for garnish

1. Insert the crisper plate into the basket and the basket into the unit. Preheat the unit by selecting AIR ROAST, setting the temperature to 204°C, and setting the time to 3 minutes. Select START/STOP to begin. 2. In a large bowl, toss together the broccoli, olive oil, salt, and pepper. 3. In a medium bowl, toss together the pork and 3 tablespoons of teriyaki sauce to coat the meat. 4. Once the unit is preheated, spray the crisper plate with olive oil. Put the broccoli and pork into the basket. Spray them with olive oil and drizzle with 1 tablespoon of teriyaki sauce. 5. Select AIR ROAST, set the temperature to 204°C, and set the time to 13 minutes. Select START/STOP to begin. 6. After 10 to 12 minutes, the broccoli is tender and light golden brown and a food thermometer inserted into the pork should register 64°C. Remove the basket and drizzle the broccoli and pork with the remaining 60 ml of teriyaki sauce and toss to coat. Reinsert the basket to resume cooking for 1 minute. 7. When the cooking is complete, serve immediately over the hot cooked rice, if desired, garnished with the sesame seeds.

Parmesan Herb Filet Mignon

Prep time: 20 minutes | Cook time: 13 minutes | Serves 4

450 g filet mignon	1 teaspoon dried rosemary
Sea salt and ground black pepper, to taste	1 teaspoon dried thyme
	1 tablespoon sesame oil
½ teaspoon cayenne pepper	1 small-sized egg, well-whisked
1 teaspoon dried basil	120 ml Parmesan cheese, grated

1. Season the filet mignon with salt, black pepper, cayenne pepper, basil, rosemary, and thyme. Brush with sesame oil. 2. Put the egg in a shallow plate. Now, place the Parmesan cheese in another plate. 3. Coat the filet mignon with the egg; then lay it into the Parmesan cheese. Set the air fryer to 182°C. 4. Cook for 10 to 13 minutes or until golden. Serve with mixed salad leaves and enjoy!

Bacon Wrapped Pork with Apple Gravy

Prep time: 10 minutes | Cook time: 25 minutes | Serves 4

Pork:	1 small shallot, chopped
1 tablespoons Dijon mustard	2 apples
1 pork tenderloin	1 tablespoon almond flour
3 strips bacon	235 ml vegetable stock
Apple Gravy:	½ teaspoon Dijon mustard
3 tablespoons ghee, divided	

1. Preheat the air fryer to 182°C. 2. Spread Dijon mustard all over tenderloin and wrap with strips of bacon. 3. Put into air fryer and air fry for 12 minutes. Use a meat thermometer to check for doneness. 4. To make sauce, heat 1 tablespoons of ghee in a pan and add shallots. Cook for 1 minute. 5. Then add apples, cooking for 4 minutes until softened. 6. Add flour and 2 tablespoons of ghee to make a roux. Add stock and mustard, stirring well to combine. 7. When sauce starts to bubble, add 235 ml of sautéed apples, cooking until sauce thickens. 8. Once pork tenderloin is cooked, allow to sit 8 minutes to rest before slicing. 9. Serve topped with apple gravy.

Zesty London Broil

Prep time: 30 minutes | Cook time: 20 to 28 minutes | Serves 4 to 6

160 ml ketchup	2 tablespoons minced onion
60 ml honey	½ teaspoon paprika
60 ml olive oil	1 teaspoon salt
2 tablespoons apple cider vinegar	1 teaspoon freshly ground black pepper
2 tablespoons Worcestershire sauce	900 g bavette or skirt steak (about 1-inch thick)

1. Combine the ketchup, honey, olive oil, apple cider vinegar, Worcestershire sauce, minced onion, paprika, salt and pepper in a small bowl and whisk together. 2. Generously pierce both sides of the meat with a fork or meat tenderizer and place it in a shallow dish. Pour the marinade mixture over the steak, making sure all sides of the meat get coated with the marinade. Cover and refrigerate overnight. 3. Preheat the air fryer to 204ºC. 4. Transfer the steak to the air fryer basket and air fry for 20 to 28 minutes, depending on how rare or well done you like your steak. Flip the steak over halfway through the cooking time. 5. Remove the steak from the air fryer and let it rest for five minutes on a cutting board. To serve, thinly slice the meat against the grain and transfer to a serving platter.

Vietnamese "Shaking" Beef

Prep time: 30 minutes | Cook time: 4 minutes per batch | Serves 4

Meat:	¼ teaspoon coarse or flaky salt
4 garlic cloves, minced	¼ teaspoon black pepper
2 teaspoons soy sauce	½ red onion, halved and very thinly sliced
2 teaspoons sugar	
1 teaspoon toasted sesame oil	1 head butterhead lettuce, leaves separated and torn into large pieces
1 teaspoon coarse or flaky salt	
¼ teaspoon black pepper	
680 g flat iron or top rump steak, cut into 1-inch cubes	120 ml halved baby plum tomatoes
Salad:	60 ml fresh mint leaves
2 tablespoons rice vinegar or apple cider vinegar	For Serving:
	Lime wedges
2 tablespoons vegetable oil	Coarse salt and freshly cracked black pepper, to taste
1 garlic clove, minced	
2 teaspoons sugar	

1. For the meat: In a small bowl, combine the garlic, soy sauce, sugar, sesame oil, salt, and pepper. Place the meat in a gallon-size resealable plastic bag. Pour the marinade over the meat. Seal and place the bag in a large bowl. Marinate for 30 minutes, or cover and refrigerate for up to 24 hours. 2. Place half the meat in the air fryer basket. Set the air fryer to 232ºC for 4 minutes, shaking the basket to redistribute the meat halfway through the cooking time. Transfer the meat to a plate (it should be medium-rare, still pink in the middle). Cover lightly with aluminum foil. Repeat to cook the remaining meat. 3. Meanwhile, for the salad: In a large bowl, whisk together the vinegar, vegetable oil, garlic, sugar, salt, and pepper. Add the onion. Stir to combine. Add the lettuce, tomatoes, and mint and toss to combine. Arrange the salad on a serving platter. 4. Arrange the cooked meat over the salad. Drizzle any accumulated juices from the plate over the meat. Serve with lime wedges, coarse salt, and cracked black pepper.

Spinach and Beef Braciole

Prep time: 25 minutes | Cook time: 1 hour 32 minutes | Serves 4

½ onion, finely chopped	680 g)
1 teaspoon olive oil	salt and freshly ground black pepper
80 ml red wine	
475 ml crushed tomatoes	475 ml fresh spinach, chopped
1 teaspoon Italian seasoning	1 clove minced garlic
½ teaspoon garlic powder	120 ml roasted red peppers, julienned
¼ teaspoon crushed red pepper flakes	
	120 ml grated pecorino cheese
2 tablespoons chopped fresh parsley	60 ml pine nuts, toasted and roughly chopped
2 bavette or skirt steaks (about	2 tablespoons olive oil

1. Preheat the air fryer to 204ºC. 2. Toss the onions and olive oil together in a baking pan or casserole dish. Air fry at 204ºC for 5 minutes, stirring a couple times during the cooking process. Add the red wine, crushed tomatoes, Italian seasoning, garlic powder, red pepper flakes and parsley and stir. Cover the pan tightly with aluminum foil, lower the air fryer temperature to 176ºC and continue to air fry for 15 minutes. 3. While the sauce is simmering, prepare the beef. Using a meat mallet, pound the beef until it is ¼-inch thick. Season both sides of the beef with salt and pepper. Combine the spinach, garlic, red peppers, pecorino cheese, pine nuts and olive oil in a medium bowl. Season with salt and freshly ground black pepper. Disperse the mixture over the steaks. Starting at one of the short ends, roll the beef around the filling, tucking in the sides as you roll to ensure the filling is completely enclosed. Secure the beef rolls with toothpicks. 4. Remove the baking pan with the sauce from the air fryer and set it aside. Preheat the air fryer to 204ºC. 5. Brush or spray the beef rolls with a little olive oil and air fry at 204ºC for 12 minutes, rotating the beef during the cooking process for even browning. When the beef is browned, submerge the rolls into the sauce in the baking pan, cover the pan with foil and return it to the air fryer. Reduce the temperature of the air fryer to 121ºC and air fry for 60 minutes. 6. Remove the beef rolls from the sauce. Cut each roll into slices and serve, ladling some sauce overtop.

Pigs in a Blanket

Prep time: 10 minutes | Cook time: 7 minutes | Serves 2

120 ml shredded Mozzarella cheese
2 tablespoons blanched finely ground almond flour
30 g full-fat cream cheese

2 (110 g) beef smoked sausage, cut in two
½ teaspoon sesame seeds

1. Place Mozzarella, almond flour, and cream cheese in a large microwave-safe bowl. Microwave for 45 seconds and stir until smooth. Roll dough into a ball and cut in half. 2. Press each half out into a 4 × 5-inch rectangle. Roll one sausage up in each dough half and press seams closed. Sprinkle the top with sesame seeds. 3. Place each wrapped sausage into the air fryer basket. 4. Adjust the temperature to 204°C and air fry for 7 minutes. 5. The outside will be golden when completely cooked. Serve immediately.

Beef Fillet with Thyme and Parsley

Prep time: 5 minutes | Cook time: 15 minutes | Serves 4

1 tablespoon butter, melted
¼ dried thyme
1 teaspoon garlic salt

¼ teaspoon dried parsley
450 g beef fillet

1. Preheat the air fryer to 204°C. 2. In a bowl, combine the melted butter, thyme, garlic salt, and parsley. 3. Cut the beef fillet into slices and generously apply the seasoned butter using a brush. Transfer to the air fryer basket. 4. Air fry the beef for 15 minutes. 5. Take care when removing it and serve hot.

Chapter 6 Fish and Seafood

Chapter 6 Fish and Seafood

Sole and Cauliflower Fritters

Prep time: 5 minutes | Cook time: 24 minutes | Serves 2

230 g sole fillets
230 g mashed cauliflower
75 g red onion, chopped
1 bell pepper, finely chopped
1 egg, beaten
2 garlic cloves, minced
2 tablespoons fresh parsley, chopped
1 tablespoon olive oil
1 tablespoon coconut aminos or tamari
½ teaspoon scotch bonnet pepper, minced
½ teaspoon paprika
Salt and white pepper, to taste
Cooking spray

1. Preheat the air fryer to 202°C. Spray the air fryer basket with cooking spray. 2. Place the sole fillets in the basket and air fry for 10 minutes, flipping them halfway through. 3. When the fillets are done, transfer them to a large bowl. Mash the fillets into flakes. Add the remaining ingredients and stir to combine. 4. Make the fritters: Scoop out 2 tablespoons of the fish mixture and shape into a patty about ½ inch thick with your hands. Repeat with the remaining fish mixture. 5. Arrange the patties in the air fryer basket and bake for 14 minutes, flipping the patties halfway through, or until they are golden brown and cooked through. 6. Cool for 5 minutes and serve on a plate.

Scallops and Spinach with Cream Sauce

Prep time: 5 minutes | Cook time: 10 minutes | Serves 2

Vegetable oil spray
280 g frozen spinach, thawed and drained
8 jumbo sea scallops
Kosher or coarse sea salt, and black pepper, to taste
180 ml heavy cream
1 tablespoon tomato paste
1 tablespoon chopped fresh basil
1 teaspoon minced garlic

1. Spray a baking pan with vegetable oil spray. Spread the thawed spinach in an even layer in the bottom of the pan. 2. Spray both sides of the scallops with vegetable oil spray. Season lightly with salt and pepper. Arrange the scallops on top of the spinach. 3. In a small bowl, whisk together the cream, tomato paste, basil, garlic, ½ teaspoon salt, and ½ teaspoon pepper. Pour the sauce over the scallops and spinach. 4. Place the pan in the air fryer basket. Set the air fryer to 176°C for 10 minutes. Use a meat thermometer to ensure the scallops have an internal temperature of 56°C.

Confetti Salmon Burgers

Prep time: 10 minutes | Cook time: 12 minutes | Serves 4

400 g cooked fresh or canned salmon, flaked with a fork
40 g minced spring onions, white and light green parts only
40 g minced red bell pepper
40 g minced celery
2 small lemons
1 teaspoon crab boil seasoning
such as Old Bay
½ teaspoon kosher or coarse sea salt
½ teaspoon black pepper
1 egg, beaten
30 g fresh bread crumbs
Vegetable oil, for spraying

1. In a large bowl, combine the salmon, vegetables, the zest and juice of 1 of the lemons, crab boil seasoning, salt, and pepper. Add the egg and bread crumbs and stir to combine. Form the mixture into 4 patties weighing approximately 140 g each. Chill until firm, about 15 minutes. 2. Preheat the air fryer to 204°C. 3. Spray the salmon patties with oil on all sides and spray the air fryer basket to prevent sticking. Air fry for 12 minutes, flipping halfway through, until the burgers are browned and cooked through. Cut the remaining lemon into 4 wedges and serve with the burgers.

Southern-Style Catfish

Prep time: 10 minutes | Cook time: 12 minutes | Serves 4

4 (200 g) catfish fillets
80 ml heavy whipping cream
1 tablespoon lemon juice
110 g blanched finely ground almond flour
2 teaspoons Old Bay seasoning
½ teaspoon salt
¼ teaspoon ground black pepper

1. Place catfish fillets into a large bowl with cream and pour in lemon juice. Stir to coat. 2. In a separate large bowl, mix flour and Old Bay seasoning. 3. Remove each fillet and gently shake off excess cream. Sprinkle with salt and pepper. Press each fillet gently into flour mixture on both sides to coat. 4. Place fillets into ungreased air fryer basket. Adjust the temperature to 204°C and air fry for 12 minutes, turning fillets halfway through cooking. Catfish will be golden brown and have an internal temperature of at least 64°C when done. Serve warm.

Smoky Prawns and Chorizo Tapas

Prep time: 15 minutes | Cook time: 10 minutes |
Serves 2 to 4

110 g Spanish (cured) chorizo, halved horizontally and sliced crosswise	1 tablespoon finely chopped fresh oregano
230 g raw medium prawns, peeled and deveined	½ teaspoon smoked Spanish paprika
1 tablespoon extra-virgin olive oil	¼ teaspoon kosher or coarse sea salt
1 small shallot, halved and thinly sliced	¼ teaspoon black pepper
1 garlic clove, minced	3 tablespoons fresh orange juice
	1 tablespoon minced fresh parsley

1. Place the chorizo in a baking pan. Set the pan in the air fryer basket. Set the air fryer to 192°C for 5 minutes, or until the chorizo has started to brown and render its fat. 2. Meanwhile, in a large bowl, combine the prawns, olive oil, shallot, garlic, oregano, paprika, salt, and pepper. Toss until the prawns are well coated. 3. Transfer the prawns to the pan with the chorizo. Stir to combine. Place the pan in the air fryer basket. Cook for 10 minutes, stirring halfway through the cooking time. 4. Transfer the prawns and chorizo to a serving dish. Drizzle with the orange juice and toss to combine. Sprinkle with the parsley.

Tandoori Prawns

Prep time: 25 minutes | Cook time: 6 minutes |
Serves 4

455 g jumbo raw prawns (21 to 25 count), peeled and deveined	1 teaspoon garam masala
1 tablespoon minced fresh ginger	1 teaspoon smoked paprika
3 cloves garlic, minced	1 teaspoon kosher or coarse sea salt
5 g chopped fresh coriander or parsley, plus more for garnish	½ to 1 teaspoon cayenne pepper
1 teaspoon ground turmeric	2 tablespoons olive oil (for Paleo) or melted ghee
	2 teaspoons fresh lemon juice

1. In a large bowl, combine the prawns, ginger, garlic, coriander, turmeric, garam masala, paprika, salt, and cayenne. Toss well to coat. Add the oil or ghee and toss again. Marinate at room temperature for 15 minutes, or cover and refrigerate for up to 8 hours. 2. Place the prawns in a single layer in the air fryer basket. Set the air fryer to 164°C for 6 minutes. Transfer the prawns to a serving platter. Cover and let the prawns finish cooking in the residual heat, about 5 minutes. 3. Sprinkle the prawns with the lemon juice and toss to coat. Garnish with additional cilantro and serve.

Panko-Crusted Fish Sticks

Prep time: 10 minutes | Cook time: 15 minutes | Serves 4

Tartar Sauce:	75 g plain flour
470 ml mayonnaise	120 g panko bread crumbs
2 tablespoons dill pickle relish	2 tablespoons Creole seasoning
1 tablespoon dried minced onions	2 teaspoons garlic granules
Fish Sticks:	1 teaspoon onion powder
Olive or vegetable oil, for spraying	½ teaspoon salt
455 g tilapia fillets	¼ teaspoon freshly ground black pepper
	1 large egg

Make the Tartar Sauce: 1. In a small bowl, whisk together the mayonnaise, pickle relish, and onions. Cover with plastic wrap and refrigerate until ready to serve. You can make this sauce ahead of time; the flavors will intensify as it chills. Make the Fish Sticks: 2. Preheat the air fryer to 176°C. Line the air fryer basket with baking paper and spray lightly with oil. 3. Cut the fillets into equal-size sticks and place them in a zip-top plastic bag. 4. Add the flour to the bag, seal, and shake well until evenly coated. 5. In a shallow bowl, mix together the bread crumbs, Creole seasoning, garlic, onion powder, salt, and black pepper. 6. In a small bowl, whisk the egg. 7. Dip the fish sticks in the egg, then dredge in the bread crumb mixture until completely coated. 8. Place the fish sticks in the prepared basket. You may need to work in batches, depending on the size of your air fryer. Do not overcrowd. Spray lightly with oil. 9. Cook for 12 to 15 minutes, or until browned and cooked through. Serve with the tartar sauce.

New Orleans-Style Crab Cakes

Prep time: 10 minutes | Cook time: 8 to 10 minutes |
Serves 4

190 g bread crumbs	360 g crab meat
2 teaspoons Creole Seasoning	2 large eggs, beaten
1 teaspoon dry mustard	1 teaspoon butter, melted
1 teaspoon salt	⅓ cup minced onion
1 teaspoon freshly ground black pepper	Cooking spray
	Tartar Sauce, for serving

1. Preheat the air fryer to 176°C. Line the air fryer basket with baking paper. 2. In a medium bowl, whisk the bread crumbs, Creole Seasoning, dry mustard, salt, and pepper until blended. Add the crab meat, eggs, butter, and onion. Stir until blended. Shape the crab mixture into 8 patties. 3. Place the crab cakes on the baking paper and spritz with oil. 4. Air fry for 4 minutes. Flip the cakes, spritz them with oil, and air fry for 4 to 6 minutes more until the outsides are firm and a fork inserted into the center comes out clean. Serve with the Tartar Sauce.

Rainbow Salmon Kebabs

Prep time: 10 minutes | Cook time: 8 minutes | Serves 2

170 g boneless, skinless salmon, cut into 1-inch cubes	½ medium courgette, trimmed and cut into ½-inch slices
¼ medium red onion, peeled and cut into 1-inch pieces	1 tablespoon olive oil
½ medium yellow bell pepper, seeded and cut into 1-inch pieces	½ teaspoon salt
	¼ teaspoon ground black pepper

1. Using one (6-inch) skewer, skewer 1 piece salmon, then 1 piece onion, 1 piece bell pepper, and finally 1 piece courgette. Repeat this pattern with additional skewers to make four kebabs total. Drizzle with olive oil and sprinkle with salt and black pepper. 2. Place kebabs into ungreased air fryer basket. Adjust the temperature to 204°C and air fry for 8 minutes, turning kebabs halfway through cooking. Salmon will easily flake and have an internal temperature of at least 64°C when done; vegetables will be tender. Serve warm.

Prawn Kebabs

Prep time: 15 minutes | Cook time: 6 minutes | Serves 4

Olive or vegetable oil, for spraying	1 tablespoon packed light brown sugar
455 g medium raw prawns, peeled and deveined	1 teaspoon granulated garlic
4 tablespoons unsalted butter, melted	1 teaspoon onion powder
1 tablespoon Old Bay seasoning	½ teaspoon freshly ground black pepper

1. Line the air fryer basket with baking paper and spray lightly with oil. 2. Thread the prawns onto the skewers and place them in the prepared basket. 3. In a small bowl, mix together the butter, Old Bay, brown sugar, garlic, onion powder, and black pepper. Brush the sauce on the prawns. 4. Air fry at 204°C for 5 to 6 minutes, or until pink and firm. Serve immediately.

Almond Catfish

Prep time: 10 minutes | Cook time: 12 minutes | Serves 4

900 g catfish fillet	1 teaspoon salt
50 g almond flour	1 teaspoon avocado oil
2 eggs, beaten	

1. Sprinkle the catfish fillet with salt and dip in the eggs. 2. Then coat the fish in the almond flour and put in the air fryer basket. Sprinkle the fish with avocado oil. 3. Cook the fish for 6 minutes per side at 192°C.

Baked Salmon with Tomatoes and Olives

Prep time: 5 minutes | Cook time: 8 minutes | Serves 4

2 tablespoons olive oil	1 teaspoon chopped fresh dill
4 (1½-inch-thick) salmon fillets	2 plum tomatoes, diced
½ teaspoon salt	45 g sliced Kalamata olives
¼ teaspoon cayenne	4 lemon slices

1. Preheat the air fryer to 192°C. 2. Brush the olive oil on both sides of the salmon fillets, and then season them lightly with salt, cayenne, and dill. 3. Place the fillets in a single layer in the basket of the air fryer, then layer the tomatoes and olives over the top. Top each fillet with a lemon slice. 4. Bake for 8 minutes, or until the salmon has reached an internal temperature of 64°C.

Tuna-Stuffed Quinoa Patties

Prep time: 10 minutes | Cook time: 15 minutes | Serves 4

35 g quinoa	2 to 3 lemons
4 slices white bread with crusts removed	Kosher or coarse sea salt, and pepper, to taste
120 ml milk	150 g panko bread crumbs
3 eggs	Vegetable oil, for spraying
280 g tuna packed in olive oil, drained	Lemon wedges, for serving

1. Rinse the quinoa in a fine-mesh sieve until the water runs clear. Bring 1 liter of salted water to a boil. Add the quinoa, cover, and reduce heat to low. Simmer the quinoa covered until most of the water is absorbed and the quinoa is tender, 15 to 20 minutes. Drain and allow to cool to room temperature. Meanwhile, soak the bread in the milk. 2. Mix the drained quinoa with the soaked bread and 2 of the eggs in a large bowl and mix thoroughly. In a medium bowl, combine the tuna, the remaining egg, and the juice and zest of 1 of the lemons. Season well with salt and pepper. Spread the panko on a plate. 3. Scoop up approximately 60 g of the quinoa mixture and flatten into a patty. Place a heaping tablespoon of the tuna mixture in the center of the patty and close the quinoa around the tuna. Flatten the patty slightly to create an oval-shaped croquette. Dredge both sides of the croquette in the panko. Repeat with the remaining quinoa and tuna. 4. Spray the air fryer basket with oil to prevent sticking, and preheat the air fryer to 204°C. Arrange 4 or 5 of the croquettes in the basket, taking care to avoid overcrowding. Spray the tops of the croquettes with oil. Air fry for 8 minutes until the top side is browned and crispy. Carefully turn the croquettes over and spray the second side with oil. Air fry until the second side is browned and crispy, another 7 minutes. Repeat with the remaining croquettes. 5. Serve the croquetas warm with plenty of lemon wedges for spritzing.

Garlic Lemon Scallops

Prep time: 5 minutes | Cook time: 10 minutes | Serves 4

4 tablespoons salted butter, melted	8 sea scallops, 30 g each, cleaned and patted dry
4 teaspoons peeled and finely minced garlic	¼ teaspoon salt
½ small lemon, zested and juiced	¼ teaspoon ground black pepper

1. In a small bowl, mix butter, garlic, lemon zest, and lemon juice. Place scallops in an ungreased round nonstick baking dish. Pour butter mixture over scallops, then sprinkle with salt and pepper. 2. Place dish into air fryer basket. Adjust the temperature to 182°C and bake for 10 minutes. Scallops will be opaque and firm, and have an internal temperature of 56°C when done. Serve warm.

Prawn Bake

Prep time: 15 minutes | Cook time: 5 minutes | Serves 4

400 g prawns, peeled and deveined	120 g Cheddar cheese, shredded
1 egg, beaten	½ teaspoon coconut oil
120 ml coconut milk	1 teaspoon ground coriander

1. In the mixing bowl, mix prawns with egg, coconut milk, Cheddar cheese, coconut oil, and ground coriander. 2. Then put the mixture in the baking ramekins and put in the air fryer. 3. Cook the prawns at 204°C for 5 minutes.

Scallops with Asparagus and Peas

Prep time: 10 minutes | Cook time: 7 to 10 minutes | Serves 4

Cooking oil spray	lemon juice
455 g asparagus, ends trimmed, cut into 2-inch pieces	2 teaspoons extra-virgin olive oil
100 g sugar snap peas	½ teaspoon dried thyme
455 g sea scallops	Salt and freshly ground black pepper, to taste
1 tablespoon freshly squeezed	

1. Insert the crisper plate into the basket and the basket into the unit. Preheat the unit to 204°C. 2. Once the unit is preheated, spray the crisper plate with cooking oil. Place the asparagus and sugar snap peas into the basket. 3. Cook for 10 minutes. 4. Meanwhile, check the scallops for a small muscle attached to the side. Pull it off and discard. In a medium bowl, toss together the scallops, lemon juice, olive oil, and thyme. Season with salt and pepper. 5. After 3 minutes, the vegetables should be just starting to get tender. Place the scallops on top of the vegetables. Reinsert the basket to resume cooking. After 3 minutes more, remove the basket and shake it. Again reinsert the basket to resume cooking. 6. When the cooking is complete, the scallops should be firm when tested with your finger and opaque in the center, and the vegetables tender. Serve immediately.

Lemony Salmon

Prep time: 30 minutes | Cook time: 10 minutes | Serves 4

680 g salmon steak	garnish
½ teaspoon grated lemon zest	120 ml dry white wine, or apple cider vinegar
Freshly cracked mixed peppercorns, to taste	½ teaspoon fresh coriander, chopped
80 ml lemon juice	Fine sea salt, to taste
Fresh chopped chives, for	

1. To prepare the marinade, place all ingredients, except for salmon steak and chives, in a deep pan. Bring to a boil over medium-high flame until it has reduced by half. Allow it to cool down. 2. After that, allow salmon steak to marinate in the refrigerator approximately 40 minutes. Discard the marinade and transfer the fish steak to the preheated air fryer. 3. Air fry at 204°C for 9 to 10 minutes. To finish, brush hot fish steaks with the reserved marinade, garnish with fresh chopped chives, and serve right away!

Prawns Scampi

Prep time: 8 minutes | Cook time: 8 minutes | Serves 4

4 tablespoons salted butter or ghee	2 tablespoons dry white wine or chicken broth
1 tablespoon fresh lemon juice	2 tablespoons chopped fresh basil, plus more for sprinkling, or 1 teaspoon dried
1 tablespoon minced garlic	
2 teaspoons red pepper flakes	
455 g prawns (21 to 25 count), peeled and deveined	1 tablespoon chopped fresh chives, or 1 teaspoon dried

1. Place a baking pan in the air fryer basket. Set the air fryer to 164°C for 8 minutes (this will preheat the pan so the butter will melt faster). 2. Carefully remove the pan from the fryer and add the butter, lemon juice, garlic, and red pepper flakes. Place the pan back in the fryer. 3. Cook for 2 minutes, stirring once, until the butter has melted. (Do not skip this step; this is what infuses the butter with garlic flavor, which is what makes it all taste so good.) 4. Carefully remove the pan from the fryer and add the prawns, broth, basil, and chives. Stir gently until the ingredients are well combined. 5. Return the pan to the air fryer and cook for 5 minutes, stirring once. 6. Thoroughly stir the prawn mixture and let it rest for 1 minute on a wire rack. (This is so the prawns cook in the residual heat rather than getting overcooked and rubbery.) 7. Stir once more, sprinkle with additional chopped fresh basil, and serve.

Simple Buttery Cod

Prep time: 5 minutes | Cook time: 8 minutes | Serves 2

2 cod fillets, 110 g each
2 tablespoons salted butter, melted

1 teaspoon Old Bay seasoning
½ medium lemon, sliced

1. Place cod fillets into a round baking dish. Brush each fillet with butter and sprinkle with Old Bay seasoning. Lay two lemon slices on each fillet. Cover the dish with foil and place into the air fryer basket. 2. Adjust the temperature to 176ºC and bake for 8 minutes. Flip halfway through the cooking time. When cooked, internal temperature should be at least 64ºC. Serve warm.

Oregano Tilapia Fingers

Prep time: 15 minutes | Cook time: 9 minutes | Serves 4

455 g tilapia fillet
60 g coconut flour
2 eggs, beaten

½ teaspoon ground paprika
1 teaspoon dried oregano
1 teaspoon avocado oil

1. Cut the tilapia fillets into fingers and sprinkle with ground paprika and dried oregano. 2. Then dip the tilapia fingers in eggs and coat in the coconut flour. 3. Sprinkle fish fingers with avocado oil and cook in the air fryer at 188ºC for 9 minutes.

Tortilla Prawn Tacos

Prep time: 10 minutes | Cook time: 6 minutes | Serves 4

Spicy Mayo:
3 tablespoons mayonnaise
1 tablespoon Louisiana-style hot pepper sauce, or Sriracha
Coriander-Lime Slaw:
180 g shredded green cabbage
½ small red onion, thinly sliced
1 small jalapeño, thinly sliced
2 tablespoons chopped fresh cilantro
Juice of 1 lime

¼ teaspoon kosher salt
Prawns:
1 large egg, beaten
1 cup crushed tortilla chips
24 jumbo prawns (about 455 g), peeled and deveined
⅛ teaspoon kosher or coarse sea salt
Cooking spray
8 corn tortillas, for serving

1. For the spicy mayo: In a small bowl, mix the mayonnaise and hot pepper sauce. 2. For the coriander-lime slaw: In a large bowl, toss together the cabbage, onion, jalapeño, coriander, lime juice, and salt to combine. Cover and refrigerate to chill. 3. For the prawns: Place the egg in a shallow bowl and the crushed tortilla chips in another. Season the prawns with the salt. Dip the prawns in the egg, then in the crumbs, pressing gently to adhere. Place on a work surface and spray both sides with oil. 4. Preheat the air fryer to 182ºC. 5. Working in batches, arrange a single layer of the prawns in the air fryer basket. Air fry for 6 minutes, flipping halfway, until golden and cooked through in the center. 6. To serve, place 2 tortillas on each plate and top each with 3 prawns. Top each taco with ¼ of the slaw, then drizzle with spicy mayo.

Crab Cake Sandwich

Prep time: 15 minutes | Cook time: 10 minutes | Serves 4

Crab Cakes:
60 g panko bread crumbs
1 large egg, beaten
1 large egg white
1 tablespoon mayonnaise
1 teaspoon Dijon mustard
5 g minced fresh parsley
1 tablespoon fresh lemon juice
½ teaspoon Old Bay seasoning
⅛ teaspoon sweet paprika
⅛ teaspoon kosher or coarse sea salt
Freshly ground black pepper, to

taste
280 g lump crab meat
Cooking spray
Cajun Mayo:
60 g mayonnaise
1 tablespoon minced dill pickle
1 teaspoon fresh lemon juice
¾ teaspoon Cajun seasoning
For Serving:
4 round lettuce leaves
4 whole wheat potato buns or gluten-free buns

1. For the crab cakes: In a large bowl, combine the panko, whole egg, egg white, mayonnaise, mustard, parsley, lemon juice, Old Bay, paprika, salt, and pepper to taste and mix well. Fold in the crab meat, being careful not to over mix. Gently shape into 4 round patties, ¾ inch thick. Spray both sides with oil. 2. Preheat the air fryer to 188ºC. 3. Working in batches, place the crab cakes in the air fryer basket. Air fry for about 10 minutes, flipping halfway, until the edges are golden. 4. Meanwhile, for the Cajun mayo: In a small bowl, combine the mayonnaise, pickle, lemon juice, and Cajun seasoning. 5. To serve: Place a lettuce leaf on each bun bottom and top with a crab cake and a generous tablespoon of Cajun mayonnaise. Add the bun top and serve.

Chilean Sea Bass with Olive Relish

Prep time: 10 minutes | Cook time: 10 minutes | Serves 2

Olive oil spray
2 (170 g) Chilean sea bass fillets or other firm-fleshed white fish
3 tablespoons extra-virgin olive oil
½ teaspoon ground cumin

½ teaspoon kosher or coarse sea salt
½ teaspoon black pepper
60 g pitted green olives, diced
10 g finely diced onion
1 teaspoon chopped capers

1. Spray the air fryer basket with the olive oil spray. Drizzle the fillets with the olive oil and sprinkle with the cumin, salt, and pepper. Place the fish in the air fryer basket. Set the air fryer to 164ºC for 10 minutes, or until the fish flakes easily with a fork. 2. Meanwhile, in a small bowl, stir together the olives, onion, and capers. 3. Serve the fish topped with the relish.

Tuna Steak

Prep time: 10 minutes | Cook time: 12 minutes | Serves 4

455 g tuna steaks, boneless and cubed	1 tablespoon avocado oil
1 tablespoon mustard	1 tablespoon apple cider vinegar

1. Mix avocado oil with mustard and apple cider vinegar. 2. Then brush tuna steaks with mustard mixture and put in the air fryer basket. 3. Cook the fish at 182°C for 6 minutes per side.

Cilantro Lime Baked Salmon

Prep time: 10 minutes | Cook time: 12 minutes | Serves 2

2 salmon fillets, 85 g each, skin removed	½ teaspoon finely minced garlic
1 tablespoon salted butter, melted	20 g sliced pickled jalapeños
1 teaspoon chilli powder	½ medium lime, juiced
	2 tablespoons chopped coriander

1. Place salmon fillets into a round baking pan. Brush each with butter and sprinkle with chilli powder and garlic. 2. Place jalapeño slices on top and around salmon. Pour half of the lime juice over the salmon and cover with foil. Place pan into the air fryer basket. 3. Adjust the temperature to 188°C and bake for 12 minutes. 4. When fully cooked, salmon should flake easily with a fork and reach an internal temperature of at least 64°C. 5. To serve, spritz with remaining lime juice and garnish with coriander.

Oyster Po'Boy

Prep time: 20 minutes | Cook time: 5 minutes | Serves 4

105 g plain flour	1 (12-inch) French baguette, quartered and sliced horizontally
40 g yellow cornmeal	
1 tablespoon Cajun seasoning	
1 teaspoon salt	Tartar Sauce, as needed
2 large eggs, beaten	150 g shredded lettuce, divided
1 teaspoon hot sauce	2 tomatoes, cut into slices
455 g pre-shucked oysters	Cooking spray

1. In a shallow bowl, whisk the flour, cornmeal, Cajun seasoning, and salt until blended. In a second shallow bowl, whisk together the eggs and hot sauce. 2. One at a time, dip the oysters in the cornmeal mixture, the eggs, and again in the cornmeal, coating thoroughly. 3. Preheat the air fryer to 204°C. Line the air fryer basket with baking paper. 4. Place the oysters on the baking paper and spritz with oil. 5. Air fry for 2 minutes. Shake the basket, spritz the oysters with oil, and air fry for 3 minutes more until lightly browned and crispy. 6. Spread each sandwich half with Tartar Sauce. Assemble the po'boys by layering each sandwich with fried oysters, ½ cup shredded lettuce, and 2 tomato slices. 7. Serve immediately.

Breaded Prawns Tacos

Prep time: 10 minutes | Cook time: 9 minutes | Makes 8 tacos

2 large eggs	dust
1 teaspoon prepared yellow mustard	For Serving:
455 g small prawns, peeled, deveined, and tails removed	8 large round lettuce leaves
	60 ml pico de gallo
45 g finely shredded Gouda or Parmesan cheese	20 g shredded purple cabbage
	1 lemon, sliced
80 g pork scratchings ground to	Guacamole (optional)

1. Preheat the air fryer to 204°C. 2. Crack the eggs into a large bowl, add the mustard, and whisk until well combined. Add the prawns and stir well to coat. 3. In a medium-sized bowl, mix together the cheese and pork scratching dust until well combined. 4. One at a time, roll the coated prawns in the pork scratching dust mixture and use your hands to press it onto each prawns. Spray the coated prawns with avocado oil and place them in the air fryer basket, leaving space between them. 5. Air fry the prawns for 9 minutes, or until cooked through and no longer translucent, flipping after 4 minutes. 6. To serve, place a lettuce leaf on a serving plate, place several prawns on top, and top with 1½ teaspoons each of pico de gallo and purple cabbage. Squeeze some lemon juice on top and serve with guacamole, if desired. 7. Store leftover prawns in an airtight container in the refrigerator for up to 3 days. Reheat in a preheated 204°C air fryer for 5 minutes, or until warmed through.

Mustard-Crusted Fish Fillets

Prep time: 5 minutes | Cook time: 8 to 11 minutes | Serves 4

5 teaspoons yellow mustard	⅛ teaspoon freshly ground black pepper
1 tablespoon freshly squeezed lemon juice	
4 sole fillets, 100 g each	1 slice whole-wheat bread, crumbled
½ teaspoon dried thyme	2 teaspoons olive oil
½ teaspoon dried marjoram	

1. In a small bowl, mix the mustard and lemon juice. Spread this evenly over the fillets. Place them in the air fryer basket. 2. In another small bowl, mix the thyme, marjoram, pepper, bread crumbs, and olive oil. Mix until combined. 3. Gently but firmly press the spice mixture onto the top of each fish fillet. 4. Bake at 160°C for 8 to 11 minutes, or until the fish reaches an internal temperature of at least 64°C on a meat thermometer and the topping is browned and crisp. Serve immediately.

Italian Tuna Roast

Prep time: 15 minutes | Cook time: 21 to 24 minutes | Serves 8

Cooking spray

1 tablespoon Italian seasoning

⅛ teaspoon ground black pepper

1 tablespoon extra-light olive oil

1 teaspoon lemon juice

1 (900 g) tuna loin, 3 to 4 inches thick

1. Spray baking dish with cooking spray and place in air fryer basket. Preheat the air fryer to 200ºC. 2. Mix together the Italian seasoning, pepper, oil, and lemon juice. 3. Using a dull table knife or butter knife, pierce top of tuna about every half inch: Insert knife into top of tuna roast and pierce almost all the way to the bottom. 4. Spoon oil mixture into each of the holes and use the knife to push seasonings into the tuna as deeply as possible. 5. Spread any remaining oil mixture on all outer surfaces of tuna. 6. Place tuna roast in baking dish and roast for 20 minutes. Check temperature with a meat thermometer. Cook for an additional 1 to 4 minutes or until temperature reaches 64ºC. 7. Remove basket from the air fryer and let tuna sit in the basket for 10 minutes.

Crustless Prawn Quiche

Prep time: 15 minutes | Cook time: 20 minutes | Serves 2

Vegetable oil

4 large eggs

120 ml single cream

110 g raw prawns, chopped

120 g shredded Parmesan or Swiss cheese

235 g chopped spring onions

1 teaspoon sweet smoked paprika

1 teaspoon Herbes de Provence

1 teaspoon black pepper

½ to 1 teaspoon kosher or coarse sea salt

1. Generously grease a baking pan with vegetable oil. (Be sure to grease the pan well, the proteins in eggs stick something fierce. Alternatively, line the bottom of the pan with baking paper cut to fit and spray the baking paper and sides of the pan generously with vegetable oil spray.) 2. In a large bowl, beat together the eggs and single cream. Add the prawns, 90 g of the cheese, the scallions, paprika, Herbes de Provence, pepper, and salt. Stir with a fork to thoroughly combine. Pour the egg mixture into the prepared pan. 3. Place the pan in the air fryer basket. Set the air fryer to 150ºC for 20 minutes. After 17 minutes, sprinkle the remaining 30 g cheese on top and cook for the remaining 3 minutes, or until the cheese has melted, the eggs are set, and a toothpick inserted into the center comes out clean. 4. Serve the quiche warm or at room temperature.

Garlic Butter Prawns Scampi

Prep time: 5 minutes | Cook time: 8 minutes | Serves 4

Sauce:

60 g unsalted butter

2 tablespoons fish stock or chicken broth

2 cloves garlic, minced

2 tablespoons chopped fresh basil leaves

1 tablespoon lemon juice

1 tablespoon chopped fresh parsley, plus more for garnish

1 teaspoon red pepper flakes

Prawns:

455 g large prawns, peeled and deveined, tails removed

Fresh basil sprigs, for garnish

1. Preheat the air fryer to 176ºC. 2. Put all the ingredients for the sauce in a baking pan and stir to incorporate. 3. Transfer the baking pan to the air fryer and air fry for 3 minutes, or until the sauce is heated through. 4. Once done, add the prawns to the baking pan, flipping to coat in the sauce. 5. Return to the air fryer and cook for another 5 minutes, or until the prawns are pink and opaque. Stir the prawns twice during cooking. 6. Serve garnished with the parsley and basil sprigs.

Chapter 7 Snacks and Appetizers

Chapter 7 Snacks and Appetizers

Sea Salt Potato Crisps

Prep time: 30 minutes | Cook time: 27 minutes | Serves 4

Oil, for spraying

4 medium yellow potatoes such as Maris Pipers

1 tablespoon oil

⅛ to ¼ teaspoon fine sea salt

1. Line the air fryer basket with parchment and spray lightly with oil. 2. Using a mandoline or a very sharp knife, cut the potatoes into very thin slices. 3. Place the slices in a bowl of cold water and let soak for about 20 minutes. 4. Drain the potatoes, transfer them to a plate lined with paper towels, and pat dry. 5. Drizzle the oil over the potatoes, sprinkle with the salt, and toss to combine. Transfer to the prepared basket. 6. Air fry at 92°C for 20 minutes. Toss the crisps, increase the heat to 204°C, and cook for another 5 to 7 minutes, until crispy.

Chilli-Brined Fried Calamari

Prep time: 20 minutes | Cook time: 8 minutes | Serves 2

1 (227 g) jar sweet or hot pickled cherry peppers

227 g calamari bodies and tentacles, bodies cut into ½-inch-wide rings

1 lemon

475 ml plain flour

Rock salt and freshly ground

black pepper, to taste

3 large eggs, lightly beaten

Cooking spray

120 ml mayonnaise

1 teaspoon finely chopped rosemary

1 garlic clove, minced

1. Drain the pickled pepper brine into a large bowl and tear the peppers into bite-size strips. Add the pepper strips and calamari to the brine and let stand in the refrigerator for 20 minutes or up to 2 hours. 2. Grate the lemon zest into a large bowl then whisk in the flour and season with salt and pepper. Dip the calamari and pepper strips in the egg, then toss them in the flour mixture until fully coated. Spray the calamari and peppers liberally with cooking spray, then transfer half to the air fryer. Air fry at 204°C, shaking the basket halfway into cooking, until the calamari is cooked through and golden brown, about 8 minutes. Transfer to a plate and repeat with the remaining pieces. 3. In a small bowl, whisk together the mayonnaise, rosemary, and garlic. Squeeze half the zested lemon to get 1 tablespoon of juice and stir it into the sauce. Season with salt and pepper. Cut the remaining zested lemon half into 4 small wedges and serve alongside the calamari, peppers, and sauce.

String Bean Fries

Prep time: 15 minutes | Cook time: 5 to 6 minutes |
Serves 4

227 g fresh green beans

2 eggs

4 teaspoons water

120 ml white flour

120 ml breadcrumbs

¼ teaspoon salt

¼ teaspoon ground black pepper

¼ teaspoon mustard powder (optional)

Oil for misting or cooking spray

1. Preheat the air fryer to 182°C. 2. Trim stem ends from green beans, wash, and pat dry. 3. In a shallow dish, beat eggs and water together until well blended. 4. Place flour in a second shallow dish. 5. In a third shallow dish, stir together the breadcrumbs, salt, pepper, and dry mustard if using. 6. Dip each bean in egg mixture, flour, egg mixture again, then breadcrumbs. 7. When you finish coating all the green beans, open air fryer and place them in basket. 8. Cook for 3 minutes. 9. Stop and mist green beans with oil or cooking spray. 10. Cook for 2 to 3 more minutes or until green beans are crispy and nicely browned.

Shishito Peppers with Herb Dressing

Prep time: 10 minutes | Cook time: 6 minutes |
Serves 2 to 4

170 g shishito or Padron peppers

1 tablespoon vegetable oil

Rock salt and freshly ground black pepper, to taste

120 ml mayonnaise

2 tablespoons finely chopped fresh basil leaves

2 tablespoons finely chopped

fresh flat-leaf parsley

1 tablespoon finely chopped fresh tarragon

1 tablespoon finely chopped fresh chives

Finely grated zest of ½ lemon

1 tablespoon fresh lemon juice

Flaky sea salt, for serving

1. Preheat the air fryer to 204°C. 2. In a bowl, toss together the shishitos and oil to evenly coat and season with rock salt and black pepper. Transfer to the air fryer and air fry for 6 minutes, shaking the basket halfway through, or until the shishitos are blistered and lightly charred. 3. Meanwhile, in a small bowl, whisk together the mayonnaise, basil, parsley, tarragon, chives, lemon zest, and lemon juice. 4. Pile the peppers on a plate, sprinkle with flaky sea salt, and serve hot with the dressing.

Crispy Green Bean Fries with Lemon-Yoghurt Sauce

Prep time: 5 minutes | Cook time: 5 minutes | Serves 4

Green Beans:	227 g whole green beans
1 egg	Lemon-Yoghurt Sauce:
2 tablespoons water	120 ml non-fat plain Greek
1 tablespoon wholemeal flour	yoghurt
¼ teaspoon paprika	1 tablespoon lemon juice
½ teaspoon garlic powder	¼ teaspoon salt
½ teaspoon salt	⅛ teaspoon cayenne pepper
60 ml wholemeal breadcrumbs	

Make the Green Beans: 1. Preheat the air fryer to 192°C. 2. In a medium shallow bowl, beat together the egg and water until frothy. 3. In a separate medium shallow bowl, whisk together the flour, paprika, garlic powder, and salt, then mix in the breadcrumbs. 4. Spray the bottom of the air fryer with cooking spray. 5. Dip each green bean into the egg mixture, then into the bread crumb mixture, coating the outside with the crumbs. Place the green beans in a single layer in the bottom of the air fryer basket. 6. Fry in the air fryer for 5 minutes, or until the breading is golden brown. Make the Lemon-Yoghurt Sauce: 7. In a small bowl, combine the yoghurt, lemon juice, salt, and cayenne. 8. Serve the green bean fries alongside the lemon-yoghurt sauce as a snack or appetizer.

Garlicky and Cheesy French Fries

Prep time: 5 minutes | Cook time: 20 to 25 minutes | Serves 4

3 medium russet or Maris Piper potatoes, rinsed, dried, and cut into thin wedges or classic fry shapes	80 ml grated Parmesan cheese
	½ teaspoon salt
	¼ teaspoon freshly ground black pepper
2 tablespoons extra-virgin olive oil	Cooking oil spray
1 tablespoon granulated garlic	2 tablespoons finely chopped fresh parsley (optional)

1. In a large bowl combine the potato wedges or fries and the olive oil. Toss to coat. 2. Sprinkle the potatoes with the granulated garlic, Parmesan cheese, salt, and pepper, and toss again. 3. Insert the crisper plate into the basket and the basket into the unit. Preheat the unit by selecting AIR FRY, setting the temperature to 204°C, and setting the time to 3 minutes. Select START/STOP to begin. 4. Once the unit is preheated, spray the crisper plate with cooking oil. Place the potatoes into the basket. 5. Select AIR FRY, set the temperature to 204°C, and set the time to 20 to 25 minutes. Select START/STOP to begin. 6. After about 10 minutes, remove the basket and shake it so the fries at the bottom come up to the top. Reinsert the basket to resume cooking. 7. When the cooking is complete, top the fries with the parsley (if using) and serve hot.

Cheese Drops

Prep time: 15 minutes | Cook time: 10 minutes per batch | Serves 8

177 ml plain flour	60 ml butter, softened
½ teaspoon rock salt	240 ml shredded extra mature
¼ teaspoon cayenne pepper	Cheddar cheese, at room
¼ teaspoon smoked paprika	temperature
¼ teaspoon black pepper	Olive oil spray
Dash garlic powder (optional)	

1. In a small bowl, combine the flour, salt, cayenne, paprika, pepper, and garlic powder, if using. 2. Using a food processor, cream the butter and cheese until smooth. Gently add the seasoned flour and process until the dough is well combined, smooth, and no longer sticky. (Or make the dough in a stand mixer fitted with the paddle attachment: Cream the butter and cheese on medium speed until smooth, then add the seasoned flour and beat at low speed until smooth.) 3. Divide the dough into 32 equal-size pieces. On a lightly floured surface, roll each piece into a small ball. 4. Spray the air fryer basket with oil spray. Arrange 16 cheese drops in the basket. Set the air fryer to 164°C for 10 minutes, or until drops are just starting to brown. Transfer to a wire rack. Repeat with remaining dough, checking for doneness at 8 minutes. 5. Cool the cheese drops completely on the wire rack. Store in an airtight container until ready to serve, or up to 1 or 2 days.

Lebanese Muhammara

Prep time: 15 minutes | Cook time: 15 minutes | Serves 6

2 large red peppers	1 teaspoon ground cumin
60 ml plus 2 tablespoons extra-virgin olive oil	1 teaspoon rock salt
	1 teaspoon red pepper flakes
240 ml walnut halves	Raw vegetables (such as
1 tablespoon agave nectar or honey	cucumber, carrots, courgette slices, or cauliflower) or toasted
1 teaspoon fresh lemon juice	pitta chips, for serving

1. Drizzle the peppers with 2 tablespoons of the olive oil and place in the air fryer basket. Set the air fryer to 204°C for 10 minutes. 2. Add the walnuts to the basket, arranging them around the peppers. Set the air fryer to 204°C for 5 minutes. 3. Remove the peppers, seal in a resealable plastic bag, and let rest for 5 to 10 minutes. Transfer the walnuts to a plate and set aside to cool. 4. Place the softened peppers, walnuts, agave, lemon juice, cumin, salt, and ½ teaspoon of the pepper flakes in a food processor and purée until smooth. 5. Transfer the dip to a serving bowl and make an indentation in the middle. Pour the remaining 60 ml olive oil into the indentation. Garnish the dip with the remaining ½ teaspoon pepper flakes. 6. Serve with vegetables or toasted pitta chips.

Bacon-Wrapped Shrimp and Jalapeño

Prep time: 20 minutes | Cook time: 26 minutes | Serves 8

24 large shrimp, peeled and deveined, about 340 g	divided
5 tablespoons barbecue sauce,	12 strips bacon, cut in half
	24 small pickled jalapeño slices

1. Toss together the shrimp and 3 tablespoons of the barbecue sauce. Let stand for 15 minutes. Soak 24 wooden toothpicks in water for 10 minutes. Wrap 1 piece bacon around the shrimp and jalapeño slice, then secure with a toothpick. 2. Preheat the air fryer to 176ºC. 3. Working in batches, place half of the shrimp in the air fryer basket, spacing them ½ inch apart. Air fry for 10 minutes. Turn shrimp over with tongs and air fry for 3 minutes more, or until bacon is golden brown and shrimp are cooked through. 4. Brush with the remaining barbecue sauce and serve.

Red Pepper Tapenade

Prep time: 5 minutes | Cook time: 5 minutes | Serves 4

1 large red pepper	and roughly chopped
2 tablespoons plus 1 teaspoon olive oil, divided	1 garlic clove, minced
120 ml Kalamata olives, pitted	½ teaspoon dried oregano
	1 tablespoon lemon juice

1. Preheat the air fryer to 192ºC. 2. Brush the outside of a whole red pepper with 1 teaspoon olive oil and place it inside the air fryer basket. Roast for 5 minutes. 3. Meanwhile, in a medium bowl combine the remaining 2 tablespoons of olive oil with the olives, garlic, oregano, and lemon juice. 4. Remove the red pepper from the air fryer, then gently slice off the stem and remove the seeds. Roughly chop the roasted pepper into small pieces. 5. Add the red pepper to the olive mixture and stir all together until combined. 6. Serve with pitta chips, crackers, or crusty bread.

Authentic Scotch Eggs

Prep time: 15 minutes | Cook time: 11 to 13 minutes | Serves 6

680 g bulk lean chicken or turkey sausage	divided
3 raw eggs, divided	120 ml plain flour
355 ml dried breadcrumbs,	6 hardboiled eggs, peeled
	Cooking oil spray

1. In a large bowl, combine the chicken sausage, 1 raw egg, and 120 ml of breadcrumbs and mix well. Divide the mixture into 6 pieces and flatten each into a long oval. 2. In a shallow bowl, beat the remaining 2 raw eggs. 3. Place the flour in a small bowl. 4. Place the remaining 240 ml of breadcrumbs in a second small bowl. 5. Roll each hardboiled egg in the flour and wrap one of the chicken sausage pieces around each egg to encircle it completely. 6. One at a time, roll the encased eggs in the flour, dip in the beaten eggs, and finally dip in the breadcrumbs to coat. 7. Insert the crisper plate into the basket and the basket into the unit. Preheat the unit by selecting AIR FRY, setting the temperature to 192ºC, and setting the time to 3 minutes. Select START/STOP to begin. 8. Once the unit is preheated, spray the crisper plate with cooking oil. Place the eggs in a single layer into the basket and spray them with oil. 9. Select AIR FRY, set the temperature to 192ºC, and set the time to 13 minutes. Select START/STOP to begin. 10. After about 6 minutes, use tongs to turn the eggs and spray them with more oil. Resume cooking for 5 to 7 minutes more, or until the chicken is thoroughly cooked and the Scotch eggs are browned. 11. When the cooking is complete, serve warm.

Black Bean Corn Dip

Prep time: 10 minutes | Cook time: 10 minutes | Serves 4

½ (425 g) can black beans, drained and rinsed	60 ml shredded low-fat Cheddar cheese
½ (425 g) can corn, drained and rinsed	½ teaspoon ground cumin
60 ml chunky salsa	½ teaspoon paprika
57 g low-fat soft white cheese	Salt and freshly ground black pepper, to taste

1. Preheat the air fryer to 164ºC. 2. In a medium bowl, mix together the black beans, corn, salsa, soft white cheese, Cheddar cheese, cumin, and paprika. Season with salt and pepper and stir until well combined. 3. Spoon the mixture into a baking dish. 4. Place baking dish in the air fryer basket and bake until heated through, about 10 minutes. 5. Serve hot.

Lemony Pear Chips

Prep time: 15 minutes | Cook time: 9 to 13 minutes | Serves 4

2 firm Bosc or Anjou pears, cut crosswise into ⅛-inch-thick slices	lemon juice
	½ teaspoon ground cinnamon
1 tablespoon freshly squeezed	⅛ teaspoon ground cardamom

1. Preheat the air fryer to 192ºC. 2. Separate the smaller stem-end pear rounds from the larger rounds with seeds. Remove the core and seeds from the larger slices. Sprinkle all slices with lemon juice, cinnamon, and cardamom. 3. Put the smaller chips into the air fryer basket. Air fry for 3 to 5 minutes, or until light golden brown, shaking the basket once during cooking. Remove from the air fryer. 4. Repeat with the larger slices, air frying for 6 to 8 minutes, or until light golden brown, shaking the basket once during cooking. 5. Remove the chips from the air fryer. Cool and serve or store in an airtight container at room temperature up for to 2 days.

Italian Rice Balls

Prep time: 20 minutes | Cook time: 10 minutes |
Makes 8 rice balls

355 ml cooked sticky rice	into tiny pieces (small enough
½ teaspoon Italian seasoning	to stuff into olives)
blend	2 eggs
¾ teaspoon salt, divided	80 ml Italian breadcrumbs
8 black olives, pitted	177 ml panko breadcrumbs
28 g Mozzarella cheese, cut	Cooking spray

1. Preheat air fryer to 200ºC. 2. Stuff each black olive with a piece of Mozzarella cheese. Set aside. 3. In a bowl, combine the cooked sticky rice, Italian seasoning blend, and ½ teaspoon of salt and stir to mix well. Form the rice mixture into a log with your hands and divide it into 8 equal portions. Mould each portion around a black olive and roll into a ball. 4. Transfer to the freezer to chill for 10 to 15 minutes until firm. 5. In a shallow dish, place the Italian breadcrumbs. In a separate shallow dish, whisk the eggs. In a third shallow dish, combine the panko breadcrumbs and remaining salt. 6. One by one, roll the rice balls in the Italian breadcrumbs, then dip in the whisked eggs, finally coat them with the panko breadcrumbs. 7. Arrange the rice balls in the air fryer basket and spritz both sides with cooking spray. 8. Air fry for 10 minutes until the rice balls are golden brown. Flip the balls halfway through the cooking time. 9. Serve warm.

Hush Puppies

Prep time: 45 minutes | Cook time: 10 minutes |
Serves 12

240 ml self-raising yellow	1 large egg
cornmeal	80 ml canned creamed corn
120 ml plain flour	240 ml minced onion
1 teaspoon sugar	2 teaspoons minced jalapeño
1 teaspoon salt	pepper
1 teaspoon freshly ground black	2 tablespoons olive oil, divided
pepper	

1. Thoroughly combine the cornmeal, flour, sugar, salt, and pepper in a large bowl. 2. Whisk together the egg and corn in a small bowl. Pour the egg mixture into the bowl of cornmeal mixture and stir to combine. Stir in the minced onion and jalapeño. Cover the bowl with plastic wrap and place in the refrigerator for 30 minutes. 3. Preheat the air fryer to 192ºC. Line the air fryer basket with parchment paper and lightly brush it with 1 tablespoon of olive oil. 4. Scoop out the cornmeal mixture and form into 24 balls, about 1 inch. 5. Arrange the balls in the parchment paper-lined basket, leaving space between each ball. 6. Air fry in batches for 5 minutes. Shake the basket and brush the balls with the remaining 1 tablespoon of olive oil. Continue cooking for 5 minutes until

golden brown. 7. Remove the balls (hush puppies) from the basket and serve on a plate.

Rosemary-Garlic Shoestring Fries

Prep time: 5 minutes | Cook time: 18 minutes | Serves 2

1 large russet or Maris Piper	rosemary
potato (about 340 g), scrubbed	Rock salt and freshly ground
clean, and julienned	black pepper, to taste
1 tablespoon vegetable oil	1 garlic clove, thinly sliced
Leaves from 1 sprig fresh	Flaky sea salt, for serving

1. Preheat the air fryer to 204ºC. 2. Place the julienned potatoes in a large colander and rinse under cold running water until the water runs clear. Spread the potatoes out on a double-thick layer of paper towels and pat dry. 3. In a large bowl, combine the potatoes, oil, and rosemary. Season with rock salt and pepper and toss to coat evenly. Place the potatoes in the air fryer and air fry for 18 minutes, shaking the basket every 5 minutes and adding the garlic in the last 5 minutes of cooking, or until the fries are golden brown and crisp. 4. Transfer the fries to a plate and sprinkle with flaky sea salt while they're hot. Serve immediately.

Five-Ingredient Falafel with Garlic-Yoghurt Sauce

Prep time: 5 minutes | Cook time: 15 minutes | Serves 4

Falafel:	Salt
1 (425 g) can chickpeas,	Garlic-Yoghurt Sauce:
drained and rinsed	240 ml non-fat plain Greek
120 ml fresh parsley	yoghurt
2 garlic cloves, minced	1 garlic clove, minced
½ tablespoon ground cumin	1 tablespoon chopped fresh dill
1 tablespoon wholemeal flour	2 tablespoons lemon juice

Make the Falafel: 1. Preheat the air fryer to 182ºC. 2. Put the chickpeas into a food processor. Pulse until mostly chopped, then add the parsley, garlic, and cumin and pulse for another 1 to 2 minutes, or until the ingredients are combined and turning into a dough. 3. Add the flour. Pulse a few more times until combined. The dough will have texture, but the chickpeas should be pulsed into small bits. 4. Using clean hands, roll the dough into 8 balls of equal size, then pat the balls down a bit so they are about ½-thick disks. 5. Spray the basket of the air fryer with olive oil cooking spray, then place the falafel patties in the basket in a single layer, making sure they don't touch each other. 6. Fry in the air fryer for 15 minutes. Make the garlic-yoghurt sauce 7. In a small bowl, combine the yoghurt, garlic, dill, and lemon juice. 8. Once the falafel is done cooking and nicely browned on all sides, remove them from the air fryer and season with salt. 9. Serve hot with a side of dipping sauce.

Dark Chocolate and Cranberry Granola Bars

Prep time: 5 minutes | Cook time: 15 minutes | Serves 6

475 ml certified gluten-free quick oats	3 tablespoons unsweetened shredded coconut
2 tablespoons sugar-free dark chocolate chunks	120 ml raw honey
2 tablespoons unsweetened dried cranberries	1 teaspoon ground cinnamon
	⅛ teaspoon salt
	2 tablespoons olive oil

1. Preheat the air fryer to 182ºC. Line an 8-by-8-inch baking dish with parchment paper that comes up the side so you can lift it out after cooking. 2. In a large bowl, mix together all of the ingredients until well combined. 3. Press the oat mixture into the pan in an even layer. 4. Place the pan into the air fryer basket and bake for 15 minutes. 5. Remove the pan from the air fryer and lift the granola cake out of the pan using the edges of the parchment paper. 6. Allow to cool for 5 minutes before slicing into 6 equal bars. 7. Serve immediately or wrap in plastic wrap and store at room temperature for up to 1 week.

Mushroom Tarts

Prep time: 15 minutes | Cook time: 38 minutes | Makes 15 tarts

2 tablespoons extra-virgin olive oil, divided	60 ml dry white wine
1 small white onion, sliced	1 sheet frozen puff pastry, thawed
227 g shiitake mushrooms, sliced	240 ml shredded Gruyère cheese
¼ teaspoon sea salt	Cooking oil spray
¼ teaspoon freshly ground black pepper	1 tablespoon thinly sliced fresh chives

1. Insert the crisper plate into the basket and the basket into the unit. Preheat the unit by selecting BAKE, setting the temperature to 148ºC, and setting the time to 3 minutes. Select START/STOP to begin. 2. In a heatproof bowl that fits into the basket, stir together 1 tablespoon of olive oil, the onion, and the mushrooms. 3. Once the unit is preheated, place the bowl into the basket. 4. Select BAKE, set the temperature to 148ºC, and set the time to 7 minutes. Select START/STOP to begin. 5. After about 2½ minutes, stir the vegetables. Resume cooking. After another 2½ minutes, the vegetables should be browned and tender. Season with the salt and pepper and add the wine. Resume cooking until the liquid evaporates, about 2 minutes. 6. When the cooking is complete, place the bowl on a heatproof surface. 7. Increase the air fryer temperature to 200ºC and set the time to 3 minutes. Select START/STOP to begin. 8. Unfold the puff pastry and cut it into 15 (3-by-3-inch) squares. Using a fork, pierce the dough and brush both sides with the remaining 1 tablespoon of olive oil. 9. Evenly distribute half the cheese among the puff pastry squares, leaving a ½-inch border around the edges. Divide the mushroom-onion mixture among the pastry squares and top with the remaining cheese. 10. Once the unit is preheated, spray the crisper plate with cooking oil. Working in batches, place 5 tarts into the basket; do not stack or overlap. 11. Select BAKE, set the temperature to 200ºC, and set the time to 8 minutes. Select START/STOP to begin. 12. After 6 minutes, check the tarts; if not yet golden brown, resume cooking for about 2 minutes more. 13. When the cooking is complete, remove the tarts and transfer to a wire rack to cool. Repeat steps 10, 11, and 12 with the remaining tarts. 14. Serve garnished with the chives.

Garlic-Roasted Tomatoes and Olives

Prep time: 5 minutes | Cook time: 20 minutes | Serves 6

475 ml cherry tomatoes	1 tablespoon fresh basil, minced
4 garlic cloves, roughly chopped	1 tablespoon fresh oregano, minced
½ red onion, roughly chopped	2 tablespoons olive oil
240 ml black olives	¼ to ½ teaspoon salt
240 ml green olives	

1. Preheat the air fryer to 192ºC. 2. In a large bowl, combine all of the ingredients and toss together so that the tomatoes and olives are coated well with the olive oil and herbs. 3. Pour the mixture into the air fryer basket, and roast for 10 minutes. Stir the mixture well, then continue roasting for an additional 10 minutes. 4. Remove from the air fryer, transfer to a serving bowl, and enjoy.

Polenta Fries with Chilli-Lime Mayo

Prep time: 10 minutes | Cook time: 28 minutes | Serves 4

Polenta Fries:	1 teaspoon chilli powder
2 teaspoons vegetable or olive oil	1 teaspoon chopped fresh coriander
¼ teaspoon paprika	¼ teaspoon ground cumin
450 g prepared polenta, cut into 3-inch × ½-inch strips	Juice of ½ lime
Chilli-Lime Mayo:	Salt and freshly ground black pepper, to taste
120 ml mayonnaise	

1. Preheat the air fryer to 204ºC. 2. Mix the oil and paprika in a bowl. Add the polenta strips and toss until evenly coated. 3. Transfer the polenta strips to the air fry basket and air fry for 28 minutes until the fries are golden brown, shaking the basket once during cooking. Season as desired with salt and pepper. 4. Meanwhile, whisk together all the ingredients for the chilli-lime mayo in a small bowl. 5. Remove the polenta fries from the air fryer to a plate and serve alongside the chilli-lime mayo as a dipping sauce.

Parmesan French Fries

Prep time: 10 minutes | Cook time: 15 minutes per batch | Serves 2

2 to 3 large russet or Maris Piper potatoes, peeled and cut into ½-inch sticks	½ teaspoon salt
2 teaspoons vegetable or rapeseed oil	Freshly ground black pepper, to taste
177 ml grated Parmesan cheese	1 teaspoon fresh chopped parsley

1. Bring a large saucepan of salted water to a boil on the stovetop while you peel and cut the potatoes. Blanch the potatoes in the boiling salted water for 4 minutes while you preheat the air fryer to 204°C. Strain the potatoes and rinse them with cold water. Dry them well with a clean kitchen towel. 2. Toss the dried potato sticks gently with the oil and place them in the air fryer basket. Air fry for 25 minutes, shaking the basket a few times while the fries cook to help them brown evenly. 3. Combine the Parmesan cheese, salt and pepper. With 2 minutes left on the air fryer cooking time, sprinkle the fries with the Parmesan cheese mixture. Toss the fries to coat them evenly with the cheese mixture and continue to air fry for the final 2 minutes, until the cheese has melted and just starts to brown. Sprinkle the finished fries with chopped parsley, a little more grated Parmesan cheese if you like, and serve.

Lemon Shrimp with Garlic Olive Oil

Prep time: 5 minutes | Cook time: 6 minutes | Serves 4

454 g medium shrimp, cleaned and deveined	½ teaspoon salt
60 ml plus 2 tablespoons olive oil, divided	¼ teaspoon red pepper flakes
Juice of ½ lemon	Lemon wedges, for serving (optional)
3 garlic cloves, minced and divided	Marinara sauce, for dipping (optional)

1. Preheat the air fryer to 192°C. 2. In a large bowl, combine the shrimp with 2 tablespoons of the olive oil, as well as the lemon juice, ⅓ of the minced garlic, salt, and red pepper flakes. Toss to coat the shrimp well. 3. In a small ramekin, combine the remaining 60 ml of olive oil and the remaining minced garlic. 4. Tear off a 12-by-12-inch sheet of aluminium foil. Pour the shrimp into the centre of the foil, then fold the sides up and crimp the edges so that it forms an aluminium foil bowl that is open on top. Place this packet into the air fryer basket. 5. Roast the shrimp for 4 minutes, then open the air fryer and place the ramekin with oil and garlic in the basket beside the shrimp packet. Cook for 2 more minutes. 6. Transfer the shrimp on a serving plate or platter with the ramekin of garlic olive oil on the side for dipping. You may also serve with lemon wedges and marinara sauce, if desired.

Egg Roll Pizza Sticks

Prep time: 10 minutes | Cook time: 5 minutes | Serves 4

Olive oil	24 slices turkey pepperoni or salami
8 pieces low-fat string cheese	Marinara sauce, for dipping (optional)
8 egg roll wrappers or spring roll pastry	

1. Spray the air fryer basket lightly with olive oil. Fill a small bowl with water. 2. Place each egg roll wrapper diagonally on a work surface. It should look like a diamond. 3. Place 3 slices of turkey pepperoni in a vertical line down the centre of the wrapper. 4. Place 1 Mozzarella cheese stick on top of the turkey pepperoni. 5. Fold the top and bottom corners of the egg roll wrapper over the cheese stick. 6. Fold the left corner over the cheese stick and roll the cheese stick up to resemble a spring roll. Dip a finger in the water and seal the edge of the roll 7. Repeat with the rest of the pizza sticks. 8. Place them in the air fryer basket in a single layer, making sure to leave a little space between each one. Lightly spray the pizza sticks with oil. You may need to cook these in batches. 9. Air fry at 192°C until the pizza sticks are lightly browned and crispy, about 5 minutes. 10. These are best served hot while the cheese is melted. Accompany with a small bowl of marinara sauce, if desired.

Root Veggie Chips with Herb Salt

Prep time: 10 minutes | Cook time: 8 minutes | Serves 2

1 parsnip, washed	Cooking spray
1 small beetroot, washed	Herb Salt:
1 small turnip, washed	¼ teaspoon rock salt
½ small sweet potato, washed	2 teaspoons finely chopped fresh parsley
1 teaspoon olive oil	

1. Preheat the air fryer to 182°C. 2. Peel and thinly slice the parsnip, beetroot, turnip, and sweet potato, then place the vegetables in a large bowl, add the olive oil, and toss. 3. Spray the air fryer basket with cooking spray, then place the vegetables in the basket and air fry for 8 minutes, gently shaking the basket halfway through. 4. While the chips cook, make the herb salt in a small bowl by combining the rock salt and parsley. 5. Remove the chips and place on a serving plate, then sprinkle the herb salt on top and allow to cool for 2 to 3 minutes before serving.

Chapter 8 Vegetables and Sides

Chapter 8 Vegetables and Sides

Green Peas with Mint

Prep time: 5 minutes | Cook time: 5 minutes | Serves 4

75 g shredded lettuce	1 tablespoon fresh mint,
1 (280 g) package frozen green	shredded
peas, thawed	1 teaspoon melted butter

1. Lay the shredded lettuce in the air fryer basket. 2. Toss together the peas, mint, and melted butter and spoon over the lettuce. 3. Air fry at 180°C for 5 minutes, until peas are warm and lettuce wilts.

Saltine Wax Beans

Prep time: 10 minutes | Cook time: 7 minutes | Serves 4

60 g flour	1 teaspoon sea salt flakes
1 teaspoon smoky chipotle	2 eggs, beaten
powder	55 g crushed cream crackers
½ teaspoon ground black	285 g wax beans
pepper	Cooking spray

1. Preheat the air fryer to 180°C. 2. Combine the flour, chipotle powder, black pepper, and salt in a bowl. Put the eggs in a second bowl. Put the crushed cream crackers in a third bowl. 3. Wash the beans with cold water and discard any tough strings. 4. Coat the beans with the flour mixture, before dipping them into the beaten egg. Cover them with the crushed cream crackers. 5. Spritz the beans with cooking spray. 6. Air fry for 4 minutes. Give the air fryer basket a good shake and continue to air fry for 3 minutes. Serve hot.

Spinach and Cheese Stuffed Tomatoes

Prep time: 20 minutes | Cook time: 15 minutes | Serves 2

4 ripe beefsteak tomatoes	1 (150 g) package garlic-and-
¾ teaspoon black pepper	herb Boursin cheese
½ teaspoon coarse sea salt	3 tablespoons sour cream
1 (280 g) package frozen	45 g finely grated Parmesan
chopped spinach, thawed and	cheese
squeezed dry	

1. Cut the tops off the tomatoes. Using a small spoon, carefully remove and discard the pulp. Season the insides with ½ teaspoon of the black pepper and ¼ teaspoon of the salt. Invert the tomatoes onto paper towels and allow to drain while you make the filling. 2. Meanwhile, in a medium bowl, combine the spinach, Boursin cheese, sour cream, ½ of the Parmesan, and the remaining ¼ teaspoon salt and ¼ teaspoon pepper. Stir until ingredients are well combined. Divide the filling among the tomatoes. Top with the remaining ½ of the Parmesan. 3. Place the tomatoes in the air fryer basket. Set the air fryer to 180°C for 15 minutes, or until the filling is hot.

Cheesy Loaded Broccoli

Prep time: 10 minutes | Cook time: 10 minutes | Serves 2

215 g fresh broccoli florets	60 g sour cream
1 tablespoon coconut oil	4 slices cooked sugar-free
¼ teaspoon salt	bacon, crumbled
120 g shredded sharp Cheddar	1 medium spring onion,
cheese	trimmed and sliced on the bias

1. Place broccoli into ungreased air fryer basket, drizzle with coconut oil, and sprinkle with salt. Adjust the temperature to 180°C and roast for 8 minutes. Shake basket three times during cooking to avoid burned spots. 2. Sprinkle broccoli with Cheddar and cook for 2 additional minutes. When done, cheese will be melted and broccoli will be tender. 3. Serve warm in a large serving dish, topped with sour cream, crumbled bacon, and spring onion slices.

Garlic Parmesan-Roasted Cauliflower

Prep time: 5 minutes | Cook time: 15 minutes | Serves 6

1 medium head cauliflower,	½ tablespoon salt
leaves and core removed, cut	2 cloves garlic, peeled and
into florets	finely minced
2 tablespoons salted butter,	45 g grated Parmesan cheese,
melted	divided

1. Toss cauliflower in a large bowl with butter. Sprinkle with salt, garlic, and ½ of the Parmesan. 2. Place florets into ungreased air fryer basket. Adjust the temperature to 180°C and roast for 15 minutes, shaking basket halfway through cooking. Cauliflower will be browned at the edges and tender when done. 3. Transfer florets to a large serving dish and sprinkle with remaining Parmesan. Serve warm.

Roasted Radishes with Sea Salt

Prep time: 5 minutes | Cook time: 18 minutes | Serves 4

450 g radishes, ends trimmed if needed

2 tablespoons olive oil

½ teaspoon sea salt

1. Preheat the air fryer to 180°C. 2. In a large bowl, combine the radishes with olive oil and sea salt. 3. Pour the radishes into the air fryer and roast for 10 minutes. Stir or turn the radishes over and roast for 8 minutes more, then serve.

Parmesan-Rosemary Radishes

Prep time: 5 minutes | Cook time: 15 to 20 minutes | Serves 4

1 bunch radishes, stemmed, trimmed, and quartered

1 tablespoon avocado oil

2 tablespoons finely grated fresh Parmesan cheese

1 tablespoon chopped fresh rosemary

Sea salt and freshly ground black pepper, to taste

1. Place the radishes in a medium bowl and toss them with the avocado oil, Parmesan cheese, rosemary, salt, and pepper. 2. Set the air fryer to192°C. Arrange the radishes in a single layer in the air fryer basket. Roast for 15 to 20 minutes, until golden brown and tender. Let cool for 5 minutes before serving.

Garlic Cauliflower with Tahini

Prep time: 10 minutes | Cook time: 20 minutes | Serves 4

Cauliflower:

500 g cauliflower florets (about 1 large head)

6 garlic cloves, smashed and cut into thirds

3 tablespoons vegetable oil

½ teaspoon ground cumin

½ teaspoon ground coriander

½ teaspoon coarse sea salt

Sauce:

2 tablespoons tahini (sesame paste)

2 tablespoons hot water

1 tablespoon fresh lemon juice

1 teaspoon minced garlic

½ teaspoon coarse sea salt

1. For the cauliflower: In a large bowl, combine the cauliflower florets and garlic. Drizzle with the vegetable oil. Sprinkle with the cumin, coriander, and salt. Toss until well coated. 2. Place the cauliflower in the air fryer basket. Set the air fryer to 200°C for 20 minutes, turning the cauliflower halfway through the cooking time. 3. Meanwhile, for the sauce: In a small bowl, combine the tahini, water, lemon juice, garlic, and salt. (The sauce will appear curdled at first, but keep stirring until you have a thick, creamy, smooth mixture.) 4. Transfer the cauliflower to a large serving bowl. Pour the sauce over and toss gently to coat. Serve immediately.

Sesame Carrots and Sugar Snap Peas

Prep time: 10 minutes | Cook time: 16 minutes | Serves 4

450 g carrots, peeled sliced on the bias (½-inch slices)

1 teaspoon olive oil

Salt and freshly ground black pepper, to taste

110 g honey

1 tablespoon sesame oil

1 tablespoon soy sauce

½ teaspoon minced fresh ginger

110 g sugar snap peas

1½ teaspoons sesame seeds

1. Preheat the air fryer to 180°C. 2. Toss the carrots with the olive oil, season with salt and pepper and air fry for 10 minutes, shaking the basket once or twice during the cooking process. 3. Combine the honey, sesame oil, soy sauce and minced ginger in a large bowl. Add the sugar snap peas and the air-fried carrots to the honey mixture, toss to coat and return everything to the air fryer basket. 4. Turn up the temperature to 200°C and air fry for an additional 6 minutes, shaking the basket once during the cooking process. 5. Transfer the carrots and sugar snap peas to a serving bowl. Pour the sauce from the bottom of the cooker over the vegetables and sprinkle sesame seeds over top. Serve immediately.

Crispy Lemon Artichoke Hearts

Prep time: 10 minutes | Cook time: 15 minutes | Serves 2

1 (425 g) can artichoke hearts in water, drained

1 egg

1 tablespoon water

30 g whole wheat bread crumbs

¼ teaspoon salt

¼ teaspoon paprika

½ lemon

1. Preheat the air fryer to 192°C. 2. In a medium shallow bowl, beat together the egg and water until frothy. 3. In a separate medium shallow bowl, mix together the bread crumbs, salt, and paprika. 4. Dip each artichoke heart into the egg mixture, then into the bread crumb mixture, coating the outside with the crumbs. Place the artichokes hearts in a single layer of the air fryer basket. 5. Fry the artichoke hearts for 15 minutes. 6. Remove the artichokes from the air fryer, and squeeze fresh lemon juice over the top before serving.

Easy Rosemary Green Beans

Prep time: 5 minutes | Cook time: 5 minutes | Serves 1

1 tablespoon butter, melted

2 tablespoons rosemary

½ teaspoon salt

3 cloves garlic, minced

95 g chopped green beans

1. Preheat the air fryer to 200°C. 2. Combine the melted butter with the rosemary, salt, and minced garlic. Toss in the green beans, coating them well. 3. Air fry for 5 minutes. 4. Serve immediately.

Turnip Fries

Prep time: 10 minutes | Cook time: 20 to 30 minutes | Serves 4

900 g turnip, peeled and cut into ¼ to ½-inch fries
2 tablespoons olive oil

Salt and freshly ground black pepper, to taste

1. Preheat the air fryer to 200°C. 2. In a large bowl, combine the turnip and olive oil. Season to taste with salt and black pepper. Toss gently until thoroughly coated. 3. Working in batches if necessary, spread the turnip in a single layer in the air fryer basket. Pausing halfway through the cooking time to shake the basket, air fry for 20 to 30 minutes until the fries are lightly browned and crunchy.

Polenta Casserole

Prep time: 5 minutes | Cook time: 28 to 30 minutes | Serves 4

10 fresh asparagus spears, cut into 1-inch pieces
320 g cooked polenta, cooled to room temperature
1 egg, beaten
2 teaspoons Worcestershire

sauce
½ teaspoon garlic powder
¼ teaspoon salt
2 slices emmental cheese (about 40 g)
Oil for misting or cooking spray

1. Mist asparagus spears with oil and air fry at 200°C for 5 minutes, until crisp-tender. 2. In a medium bowl, mix together the grits, egg, Worcestershire, garlic powder, and salt. 3. Spoon half of polenta mixture into a baking pan and top with asparagus. 4. Tear cheese slices into pieces and layer evenly on top of asparagus. 5. Top with remaining polenta. 6. Bake at 180°C for 23 to 25 minutes. The casserole will rise a little as it cooks. When done, the top will have browned lightly with just a hint of crispiness.

Garlic Herb Radishes

Prep time: 10 minutes | Cook time: 10 minutes | Serves 4

450 g radishes
2 tablespoons unsalted butter, melted
½ teaspoon garlic powder

½ teaspoon dried parsley
¼ teaspoon dried oregano
¼ teaspoon ground black pepper

1. Remove roots from radishes and cut into quarters. 2. In a small bowl, add butter and seasonings. Toss the radishes in the herb butter and place into the air fryer basket. 3. Adjust the temperature to 180°C and set the timer for 10 minutes. 4. Halfway through the cooking time, toss the radishes in the air fryer basket. Continue cooking until edges begin to turn brown. 5. Serve warm.

Crispy Garlic Sliced Aubergine

Prep time: 5 minutes | Cook time: 25 minutes | Serves 4

1 egg
1 tablespoon water
60 g whole wheat bread crumbs
1 teaspoon garlic powder
½ teaspoon dried oregano

½ teaspoon salt
½ teaspoon paprika
1 medium aubergine, sliced into ¼-inch-thick rounds
1 tablespoon olive oil

1. Preheat the air fryer to 180°C. 2. In a medium shallow bowl, beat together the egg and water until frothy. 3. In a separate medium shallow bowl, mix together bread crumbs, garlic powder, oregano, salt, and paprika. 4. Dip each aubergine slice into the egg mixture, then into the bread crumb mixture, coating the outside with crumbs. Place the slices in a single layer in the bottom of the air fryer basket. 5. Drizzle the tops of the aubergine slices with the olive oil, then fry for 15 minutes. Turn each slice and cook for an additional 10 minutes.

Crispy Chickpeas

Prep time: 5 minutes | Cook time: 15 minutes | Serves 4

1 (425 g) can chickpeas, drained but not rinsed
2 tablespoons olive oil

1 teaspoon salt
2 tablespoons lemon juice

1. Preheat the air fryer to 200°C. 2. Add all the ingredients together in a bowl and mix. Transfer this mixture to the air fryer basket. 3. Air fry for 15 minutes, ensuring the chickpeas become nice and crispy. 4. Serve immediately.

Garlic Roasted Broccoli

Prep time: 8 minutes | Cook time: 10 to 14 minutes | Serves 6

1 head broccoli, cut into bite-size florets
1 tablespoon avocado oil
2 teaspoons minced garlic
⅛ teaspoon red pepper flakes

Sea salt and freshly ground black pepper, to taste
1 tablespoon freshly squeezed lemon juice
½ teaspoon lemon zest

1. In a large bowl, toss together the broccoli, avocado oil, garlic, red pepper flakes, salt, and pepper. 2. Set the air fryer to 192°C. Arrange the broccoli in a single layer in the air fryer basket, working in batches if necessary. Roast for 10 to 14 minutes, until the broccoli is lightly charred. 3. Place the florets in a medium bowl and toss with the lemon juice and lemon zest. Serve.

Balsamic Brussels Sprouts

Prep time: 5 minutes | Cook time: 12 minutes | Serves 4

180 g trimmed and halved fresh Brussels sprouts	pepper
2 tablespoons olive oil	2 tablespoons balsamic vinegar
¼ teaspoon salt	2 slices cooked sugar-free bacon, crumbled
¼ teaspoon ground black	

1. In a large bowl, toss Brussels sprouts in olive oil, then sprinkle with salt and pepper. Place into ungreased air fryer basket. Adjust the temperature to 192°C and set the timer for 12 minutes, shaking the basket halfway through cooking. Brussels sprouts will be tender and browned when done. 2. Place sprouts in a large serving dish and drizzle with balsamic vinegar. Sprinkle bacon over top. Serve warm.

Caramelized Aubergine with Harissa Yogurt

Prep time: 10 minutes | Cook time: 15 minutes | Serves 2

1 medium aubergine (about 340 g), cut crosswise into ½-inch-thick slices and quartered	ground black pepper, to taste
	120 g plain yogurt (not Greek)
2 tablespoons vegetable oil	2 tablespoons harissa paste
coarse sea salt and freshly	1 garlic clove, grated
	2 teaspoons honey

1. In a bowl, toss together the aubergine and oil, season with salt and pepper, and toss to coat evenly. Transfer to the air fryer and air fry at 200°C, shaking the basket every 5 minutes, until the aubergine is caramelized and tender, about 15 minutes. 2. Meanwhile, in a small bowl, whisk together the yogurt, harissa, and garlic, then spread onto a serving plate. 3. Pile the warm aubergine over the yogurt and drizzle with the honey just before serving.

Cauliflower Steaks Gratin

Prep time: 10 minutes | Cook time: 13 minutes | Serves 2

1 head cauliflower	thyme leaves
1 tablespoon olive oil	3 tablespoons grated
Salt and freshly ground black pepper, to taste	Parmigiano-Reggiano cheese
½ teaspoon chopped fresh	2 tablespoons panko bread crumbs

1. Preheat the air fryer to 192°C. 2. Cut two steaks out of the centre of the cauliflower. To do this, cut the cauliflower in half and then cut one slice about 1-inch thick off each half. The rest of the cauliflower will fall apart into florets, which you can roast on their own or save for another meal. 3. Brush both sides of the cauliflower steaks with olive oil and season with salt, freshly ground black pepper and fresh thyme. Place the cauliflower steaks into the air fryer basket and air fry for 6 minutes. Turn the steaks over and air fry for another 4 minutes. Combine the Parmesan cheese and panko bread crumbs and sprinkle the mixture over the tops of both steaks and air fry for another 3 minutes until the cheese has melted and the bread crumbs have browned. Serve this with some sautéed bitter greens and air-fried blistered tomatoes.

Parmesan Mushrooms

Prep time: 5 minutes | Cook time: 15 minutes | Serves 4

Oil, for spraying	½ teaspoon salt
450 g shitake mushrooms, stems trimmed	¼ teaspoon freshly ground black pepper
2 tablespoons olive oil	30 g grated Parmesan cheese, divided
2 teaspoons granulated garlic	
1 teaspoon onion powder	

1. Line the air fryer basket with parchment and spray lightly with oil. 2. In a large bowl, toss the mushrooms with the olive oil, garlic, onion powder, salt, and black pepper until evenly coated. 3. Place the mushrooms in the prepared basket. 4. Roast at 192°C for 13 minutes. 5. Sprinkle half of the cheese over the mushrooms and cook for another 2 minutes. 6. Transfer the mushrooms to a serving bowl, add the remaining Parmesan cheese, and toss until evenly coated. Serve immediately.

Asian Tofu Salad

Prep time: 25 minutes | Cook time: 15 minutes | Serves 2

Tofu:	1 tablespoon sugar
1 tablespoon soy sauce	1 teaspoon salt
1 tablespoon vegetable oil	1 teaspoon black pepper
1 teaspoon minced fresh ginger	25 g sliced spring onions
1 teaspoon minced garlic	120 g julienned cucumber
230 g extra-firm tofu, drained and cubed	50 g julienned red onion
	130 g julienned carrots
Salad:	6 butter lettuce leaves
60 ml rice vinegar	

1. For the tofu: In a small bowl, whisk together the soy sauce, vegetable oil, ginger, and garlic. Add the tofu and mix gently. Let stand at room temperature for 10 minutes. 2. Arrange the tofu in a single layer in the air fryer basket. Set the air fryer to 200°C for 15 minutes, shaking halfway through the cooking time. 3. Meanwhile, for the salad: In a large bowl, whisk together the vinegar, sugar, salt, pepper, and spring onions. Add the cucumber, onion, and carrots and toss to combine. Set aside to marinate while the tofu cooks. 4. To serve, arrange three lettuce leaves on each of two plates. Pile the marinated vegetables (and marinade) on the lettuce. Divide the tofu between the plates and serve.

Buttery Mushrooms

Prep time: 10 minutes | Cook time: 10 minutes | Serves 4

230 g shitake mushrooms, halved	¼ teaspoon salt
2 tablespoons salted butter, melted	¼ teaspoon ground black pepper

1. In a medium bowl, toss mushrooms with butter, then sprinkle with salt and pepper. Place into ungreased air fryer basket. Adjust the temperature to 200°Cand air fry for 10 minutes, shaking the basket halfway through cooking. Mushrooms will be tender when done. Serve warm.

Sausage-Stuffed Mushroom Caps

Prep time: 10 minutes | Cook time: 8 minutes | Serves 2

6 large portobello mushroom caps	2 tablespoons blanched finely ground almond flour
230 g Italian sausage	20 g grated Parmesan cheese
15 g chopped onion	1 teaspoon minced fresh garlic

1. Use a spoon to hollow out each mushroom cap, reserving scrapings. 2. In a medium skillet over medium heat, brown the sausage about 10 minutes or until fully cooked and no pink remains. Drain and then add reserved mushroom scrapings, onion, almond flour, Parmesan, and garlic. Gently fold ingredients together and continue cooking an additional minute, then remove from heat. 3. Evenly spoon the mixture into mushroom caps and place the caps into a 6-inch round pan. Place pan into the air fryer basket. 4. Adjust the temperature to 192°C and set the timer for 8 minutes. 5. When finished cooking, the tops will be browned and bubbling. Serve warm.

Hasselback Potatoes with Chive Pesto

Prep time: 10 minutes | Cook time: 40 minutes | Serves 2

2 medium Maris Piper potatoes	leaf parsley leaves
5 tablespoons olive oil	1 tablespoon chopped walnuts
coarse sea salt and freshly ground black pepper, to taste	1 tablespoon grated Parmesan cheese
10 g roughly chopped fresh chives	1 teaspoon fresh lemon juice
2 tablespoons packed fresh flat-	1 small garlic clove, peeled
	60 g sour cream

1. Place the potatoes on a cutting board and lay a chopstick or thin-handled wooden spoon to the side of each potato. Thinly slice the potatoes crosswise, letting the chopstick or spoon handle stop the blade of your knife, and stop ½ inch short of each end of the potato. Rub the potatoes with 1 tablespoon of the olive oil and season with salt and pepper. 2. Place the potatoes, cut-side up,

in the air fryer and air fry at 192°C until golden brown and crisp on the outside and tender inside, about 40 minutes, drizzling the insides with 1 tablespoon more olive oil and seasoning with more salt and pepper halfway through. 3. Meanwhile, in a small blender or food processor, combine the remaining 3 tablespoons olive oil, the chives, parsley, walnuts, Parmesan, lemon juice, and garlic and purée until smooth. Season the chive pesto with salt and pepper. 4. Remove the potatoes from the air fryer and transfer to plates. Drizzle the potatoes with the pesto, letting it drip down into the grooves, then dollop each with sour cream and serve hot.

Southwestern Roasted Corn

Prep time: 10 minutes | Cook time: 10 minutes | Serves 4

Corn:	½ teaspoon ancho chili powder
240 g thawed frozen corn kernels	½ teaspoon coarse sea salt
50 g diced yellow onion	For Serving:
150 g mixed diced bell peppers	150 g queso fresco or feta cheese
1 jalapeño, diced	10 g chopped fresh coriander
1 tablespoon fresh lemon juice	1 tablespoon fresh lemon juice
1 teaspoon ground cumin	

1. For the corn: In a large bowl, stir together the corn, onion, bell peppers, jalapeño, lemon juice, cumin, chili powder, and salt until well incorporated. 2. Pour the spiced vegetables into the air fryer basket. Set the air fryer to 192°C for 10 minutes, stirring halfway through the cooking time. 3. Transfer the corn mixture to a serving bowl. Add the cheese, coriander, and lemon juice and stir well to combine. Serve immediately.

Asparagus Fries

Prep time: 15 minutes | Cook time: 5 to 7 minutes per batch | Serves 4

340 g fresh asparagus spears with tough ends trimmed off	25 g grated Parmesan cheese, plus 2 tablespoons
2 egg whites	¼ teaspoon salt
60 ml water	Oil for misting or cooking spray
80 g panko bread crumbs	

1. Preheat the air fryer to 200°C. 2. In a shallow dish, beat egg whites and water until slightly foamy. 3. In another shallow dish, combine panko, Parmesan, and salt. 4. Dip asparagus spears in egg, then roll in crumbs. Spray with oil or cooking spray. 5. Place a layer of asparagus in air fryer basket, leaving just a little space in between each spear. Stack another layer on top, crosswise. Air fry at 200°C for 5 to 7 minutes, until crispy and golden brown. 6. Repeat to cook remaining asparagus.

Mexican Corn in a Cup

Prep time: 5 minutes | Cook time: 10 minutes | Serves 4

650 g frozen corn kernels (do not thaw)
Vegetable oil spray
2 tablespoons butter
60 g sour cream
60 g mayonnaise

20 g grated Parmesan cheese (or feta, cotija, or queso fresco)
2 tablespoons fresh lemon or lime juice
1 teaspoon chili powder
Chopped fresh green onion (optional)
Chopped fresh coriander (optional)

1. Place the corn in the bottom of the air fryer basket and spray with vegetable oil spray. Set the air fryer to 180°C for 10 minutes. 2. Transfer the corn to a serving bowl. Add the butter and stir until melted. Add the sour cream, mayonnaise, cheese, lemon juice, and chili powder; stir until well combined. Serve immediately with green onion and coriander (if using).

Hawaiian Brown Rice

Prep time: 10 minutes | Cook time: 12 to 16 minutes | Serves 4 to 6

110 g ground sausage
1 teaspoon butter
20 g minced onion

40 g minced bell pepper
380 g cooked brown rice
1 (230 g) can crushed pineapple, drained

1. Shape sausage into 3 or 4 thin patties. Air fry at 200°C for 6 to 8 minutes or until well done. Remove from air fryer, drain, and crumble. Set aside. 2. Place butter, onion, and bell pepper in baking pan. Roast at 200°C for 1 minute and stir. Cook 3 to 4 minutes longer or just until vegetables are tender. 3. Add sausage, rice, and pineapple to vegetables and stir together. 4. Roast for 2 to 3 minutes, until heated through.

Sweet and Crispy Roasted Pearl Onions

Prep time: 5 minutes | Cook time: 18 minutes | Serves 3

1 (410 g) package frozen pearl onions (do not thaw)
2 tablespoons extra-virgin olive oil
2 tablespoons balsamic vinegar

2 teaspoons finely chopped fresh rosemary
½ teaspoon coarse sea salt
¼ teaspoon black pepper

1. In a medium bowl, combine the onions, olive oil, vinegar, rosemary, salt, and pepper until well coated. 2. Transfer the onions to the air fryer basket. Set the air fryer to 200°C for 18 minutes, or until the onions are tender and lightly charred, stirring once or twice during the cooking time.

Chapter 9 Vegetarian Mains

Chapter 9 Vegetarian Mains

Cauliflower, Chickpea, and Avocado Mash

Prep time: 10 minutes | Cook time: 25 minutes | Serves 4

1 medium head cauliflower, cut into florets
1 can chickpeas, drained and rinsed
1 tablespoon extra-virgin olive oil
2 tablespoons lemon juice
Salt and ground black pepper, to taste
4 flatbreads, toasted
2 ripe avocados, mashed

Preheat the air fryer to 218°C. In a bowl, mix the chickpeas, cauliflower, lemon juice and olive oil. Sprinkle salt and pepper as desired. Put inside the air fryer basket and air fry for 25 minutes. Spread on top of the flatbread along with the mashed avocado. Sprinkle with more pepper and salt and serve.

Buffalo Cauliflower Bites with Blue Cheese

Prep time: 10 minutes | Cook time: 8 to 10 minutes | Serves 4

1 large head cauliflower, chopped into florets
1 tablespoon olive oil
Salt and freshly ground black pepper, to taste
60 ml unsalted butter, melted
60 ml hot sauce
Garlic Blue Cheese Dip:
120 ml mayonnaise
60 ml sour cream
2 tablespoons double cream
1 tablespoon fresh lemon juice
1 clove garlic, minced
60 ml crumbled blue cheese
Salt and freshly ground black pepper, to taste

Preheat the air fryer to 204°C. In a large bowl, combine the cauliflower and olive oil. Season to taste with salt and black pepper. Toss until the vegetables are thoroughly coated. Working in batches, place half of the cauliflower in the air fryer basket. Pausing halfway through the cooking time to shake the basket, air fry for 8 to 10 minutes until the cauliflower is evenly browned. Transfer to a large bowl and repeat with the remaining cauliflower. In a small bowl, whisk together the melted butter and hot sauce. To make the dip: In a small bowl, combine the mayonnaise, sour cream, double cream, lemon juice, garlic, and blue cheese. Season to taste with salt and freshly ground black pepper. Just before serving, pour the butter mixture over the cauliflower and toss gently until thoroughly coated. Serve with the dip on the side.

Three-Cheese Courgette Boats

Prep time: 15 minutes | Cook time: 20 minutes | Serves 2

2 medium courgette
1 tablespoon avocado oil
60 ml low-carb, no-sugar-added pasta sauce
60 ml full-fat ricotta cheese
60 ml shredded Mozzarella
cheese
¼ teaspoon dried oregano
¼ teaspoon garlic powder
½ teaspoon dried parsley
2 tablespoons grated vegetarian Parmesan cheese

Cut off 1 inch from the top and bottom of each courgette. Slice courgette in half lengthwise and use a spoon to scoop out a bit of the inside, making room for filling. Brush with oil and spoon 2 tablespoons pasta sauce into each shell. In a medium bowl, mix ricotta, Mozzarella, oregano, garlic powder, and parsley. Spoon the mixture into each courgette shell. Place stuffed courgette shells into the air fryer basket. Adjust the temperature to 176°C and air fry for 20 minutes. To remove from the basket, use tongs or a spatula and carefully lift out. Top with Parmesan. Serve immediately.

Spinach-Artichoke Stuffed Mushrooms

Prep time: 10 minutes | Cook time: 10 to 14 minutes | Serves 4

2 tablespoons olive oil
4 large portobello mushrooms, stems removed and gills scraped out
½ teaspoon salt
¼ teaspoon freshly ground pepper
110 g goat cheese, crumbled
120 ml chopped marinated artichoke hearts
235 ml frozen spinach, thawed and squeezed dry
120 ml grated Parmesan cheese
2 tablespoons chopped fresh parsley

Preheat the air fryer to 204°C. Rub the olive oil over the portobello mushrooms until thoroughly coated. Sprinkle both sides with the salt and black pepper. Place top-side down on a clean work surface. In a small bowl, combine the goat cheese, artichoke hearts, and spinach. Mash with the back of a fork until thoroughly combined. Divide the cheese mixture among the mushrooms and sprinkle with the Parmesan cheese. Air fry for 10 to 14 minutes until the mushrooms are tender and the cheese has begun to brown. Top with the fresh parsley just before serving.

Black Bean and Tomato Chilli

Prep time: 15 minutes | Cook time: 23 minutes | Serves 6

1 tablespoon olive oil	2 cans diced tomatoes
1 medium onion, diced	2 chipotle peppers, chopped
3 garlic cloves, minced	2 teaspoons cumin
235 ml vegetable broth	2 teaspoons chilli powder
3 cans black beans, drained and rinsed	1 teaspoon dried oregano
	½ teaspoon salt

Over a medium heat, fry the garlic and onions in the olive oil for 3 minutes. Add the remaining ingredients, stirring constantly and scraping the bottom to prevent sticking. Preheat the air fryer to 204°C. Take a dish and place the mixture inside. Put a sheet of aluminium foil on top. Transfer to the air fryer and bake for 20 minutes. When ready, plate up and serve immediately.

Gold Ravioli

Prep time: 10 minutes | Cook time: 6 minutes | Serves 4

120 ml panko breadcrumbs	Salt and ground black pepper, to taste
2 teaspoons Engevita yeast flakes	60 ml aquafaba or egg alternative
1 teaspoon dried basil	
1 teaspoon dried oregano	227 g ravioli
1 teaspoon garlic powder	Cooking spray

Cover the air fryer basket with aluminium foil and coat with a light brushing of oil. Preheat the air fryer to 204°C. Combine the panko breadcrumbs, Engevita yeast flakes, basil, oregano, and garlic powder. Sprinkle with salt and pepper to taste. Put the aquafaba in a separate bowl. Dip the ravioli in the aquafaba before coating it in the panko mixture. Spritz with cooking spray and transfer to the air fryer. Air fry for 6 minutes. Shake the air fryer basket halfway. Serve hot.

Lush Vegetables Roast

Prep time: 15 minutes | Cook time: 20 minutes | Serves 6

315 ml small parsnips, peeled and cubed	1 tablespoon fresh thyme needles
315 ml celery	1 tablespoon olive oil
2 red onions, sliced	Salt and ground black pepper, to taste
315 ml small butternut squash, cut in half, deseeded and cubed	

Preheat the air fryer to 200°C. Combine the cut vegetables with the thyme, olive oil, salt and pepper. Put the vegetables in the basket and transfer the basket to the air fryer. Roast for 20 minutes, stirring once throughout the roasting time, until the vegetables are nicely browned and cooked through. Serve warm.

Baked Turnip and Courgette

Prep time: 5 minutes | Cook time: 15 to 20 minutes | Serves 4

3 turnips, sliced	2 cloves garlic, crushed
1 large courgette, sliced	1 tablespoon olive oil
1 large red onion, cut into rings	Salt and black pepper, to taste

Preheat the air fryer to 166°C. Put the turnips, courgette, red onion, and garlic in a baking pan. Drizzle the olive oil over the top and sprinkle with the salt and pepper. Place the baking pan in the preheated air fryer and bake for 15 to 20 minutes, or until the vegetables are tender. Remove from the basket and serve on a plate.

Teriyaki Cauliflower

Prep time: 5 minutes | Cook time: 14 minutes | Serves 4

120 ml soy sauce	2 cloves garlic, chopped
80 ml water	½ teaspoon chilli powder
1 tablespoon brown sugar	1 big cauliflower head, cut into florets
1 teaspoon sesame oil	
1 teaspoon cornflour	

Preheat the air fryer to 172°C. Make the teriyaki sauce: In a small bowl, whisk together the soy sauce, water, brown sugar, sesame oil, cornflour, garlic, and chilli powder until well combined. Place the cauliflower florets in a large bowl and drizzle the top with the prepared teriyaki sauce and toss to coat well. Put the cauliflower florets in the air fryer basket and air fry for 14 minutes, shaking the basket halfway through, or until the cauliflower is crisp-tender. Let the cauliflower cool for 5 minutes before serving.

Super Veg Rolls

Prep time: 20 minutes | Cook time: 10 minutes | Serves 6

2 potatoes, mashed	1 small onion, chopped
60 ml peas	120 ml breadcrumbs
60 ml mashed carrots	1 packet spring roll sheets
1 small cabbage, sliced	120 ml cornflour slurry (mix 40 ml cornflour with 80 ml water)
60 ml beans	
2 tablespoons sweetcorn	

Preheat the air fryer to 200°C. Boil all the vegetables in water over a low heat. Rinse and allow to dry. Unroll the spring roll sheets and spoon equal amounts of vegetable onto the centre of each one. Fold into spring rolls and coat each one with the slurry and breadcrumbs. Air fry the rolls in the preheated air fryer for 10 minutes. Serve warm.

Quiche-Stuffed Peppers

Prep time: 5 minutes | Cook time: 15 minutes | Serves 2

2 medium green peppers
3 large eggs
60 ml full-fat ricotta cheese
60 ml diced brown onion
120 ml chopped broccoli
120 ml shredded medium
Cheddar cheese

Cut the tops off of the peppers and remove the seeds and white membranes with a small knife. In a medium bowl, whisk eggs and ricotta. Add onion and broccoli. Pour the egg and vegetable mixture evenly into each pepper. Top with Cheddar. Place peppers into a 1 L round baking dish and place into the air fryer basket. Adjust the temperature to 176°C and bake for 15 minutes. Eggs will be mostly firm and peppers tender when fully cooked. Serve immediately.

Crustless Spinach Cheese Pie

Prep time: 10 minutes | Cook time: 20 minutes | Serves 4

6 large eggs
60 ml double cream
235 ml frozen chopped spinach, drained
235 ml shredded sharp Cheddar cheese
60 ml diced brown onion

In a medium bowl, whisk eggs and add cream. Add remaining ingredients to bowl. Pour into a round baking dish. Place into the air fryer basket. Adjust the temperature to 160°C and bake for 20 minutes. Eggs will be firm and slightly browned when cooked. Serve immediately.

Courgette-Ricotta Tart

Prep time: 15 minutes | Cook time: 60 minutes | Serves 6

120 ml grated Parmesan cheese, divided
350 ml almond flour
1 tablespoon coconut flour
½ teaspoon garlic powder
¾ teaspoon salt, divided
60 ml unsalted butter, melted
1 courgette, thinly sliced (about 475 ml)
235 ml ricotta cheese
3 eggs
2 tablespoons double cream
2 cloves garlic, minced
½ teaspoon dried tarragon

Preheat the air fryer to 166°C. Coat a round pan with olive oil and set aside. In a large bowl, whisk 60 ml Parmesan with the almond flour, coconut flour, garlic powder, and ¼ teaspoon of the salt. Stir in the melted butter until the dough resembles coarse crumbs. Press the dough firmly into the bottom and up the sides of the prepared pan. Air fry for 12 to 15 minutes until the crust begins to brown. Let cool to room temperature. Meanwhile, place the courgette in a colander and sprinkle with the remaining ½ teaspoon salt. Toss gently to distribute the salt and let sit for 30 minutes. Use paper towels to pat the courgette dry. In a large bowl, whisk together the ricotta, eggs, double cream, garlic, and tarragon. Gently stir in the courgette slices. Pour the cheese mixture into the cooled crust and sprinkle with the remaining 60 ml Parmesan. Increase the air fryer to 176°C. Place the pan in the air fryer basket and air fry for 45 to 50 minutes, or until set and a tester inserted into the centre of the tart comes out clean. Serve warm or at room temperature.

Garlicky Sesame Carrots

Prep time: 5 minutes | Cook time: 16 minutes |
Serves 4 to 6

450 g baby carrots
1 tablespoon sesame oil
½ teaspoon dried dill
Pinch salt
Freshly ground black pepper, to taste
6 cloves garlic, peeled
3 tablespoons sesame seeds

Preheat the air fryer to 192°C. In a medium bowl, drizzle the baby carrots with the sesame oil. Sprinkle with the dill, salt, and pepper and toss to coat well. Place the baby carrots in the air fryer basket and roast for 8 minutes. Remove the basket and stir in the garlic. Return the basket to the air fryer and roast for another 8 minutes, or until the carrots are lightly browned. Serve sprinkled with the sesame seeds.

Cauliflower Steak with Gremolata

Prep time: 15 minutes | Cook time: 25 minutes | Serves 4

2 tablespoons olive oil
1 tablespoon Italian seasoning
1 large head cauliflower, outer leaves removed and sliced lengthwise through the core into thick "steaks"
Salt and freshly ground black pepper, to taste
60 ml Parmesan cheese
Gremolata:
1 bunch Italian parsley
2 cloves garlic
Zest of 1 small lemon, plus 1 to 2 teaspoons lemon juice
120 ml olive oil
Salt and pepper, to taste

Preheat the air fryer to 204°C. In a small bowl, combine the olive oil and Italian seasoning. Brush both sides of each cauliflower "steak" generously with the oil. Season to taste with salt and black pepper. Working in batches if necessary, arrange the cauliflower in a single layer in the air fryer basket. Pausing halfway through the cooking time to turn the "steaks," air fry for 15 to 20 minutes until the cauliflower is tender and the edges begin to brown. Sprinkle with the Parmesan and air fry for 5 minutes longer. To make the gremolata: In a food processor fitted with a metal blade, combine the parsley, garlic, and lemon zest and juice. With the motor running, add the olive oil in a steady stream until the mixture forms a bright green sauce. Season to taste with salt and black pepper. Serve the cauliflower steaks with the gremolata spooned over the top.

Chapter 10 Desserts

Chapter 10 Desserts

Cream-Filled Sponge Cakes

Prep time: 10 minutes | Cook time: 10 minutes |
Makes 4 cakes

Coconut, or avocado oil, for spraying	4 cream-filled sponge cake fingers
1 tube croissant dough	1 tablespoon icing sugar

1. Line the air fryer basket with baking paper, and spray lightly with oil. 2. Unroll the dough into a single flat layer and cut it into 4 equal pieces. 3. Place 1 sponge cake in the center of each piece of dough. Wrap the dough around the cake, pinching the ends to seal. 4. Place the wrapped cakes in the prepared basket, and spray lightly with oil. 5. Bake at 92ºC for 5 minutes, flip, spray with oil, and cook for another 5 minutes, or until golden brown. 6. Dust with the icing sugar and serve.

Crumbly Coconut-Pecan Cookies

Prep time: 10 minutes | Cook time: 25 minutes |
Serves 10

170 g coconut flour	150 g monk fruit, or equivalent sweetener
170 g extra-fine almond flour	
½ teaspoon baking powder	¼ teaspoon freshly grated nutmeg
⅓ teaspoon baking soda	
3 eggs plus an egg yolk, beaten	⅓ teaspoon ground cloves
175 ml coconut oil, at room temperature	½ teaspoon pure vanilla extract
	½ teaspoon pure coconut extract
125 g unsalted pecan nuts, roughly chopped	⅛ teaspoon fine sea salt

1. Preheat the air fryer to 188ºC. Line the air fryer basket with baking paper. 2. Mix the coconut flour, almond flour, baking powder, and baking soda in a large mixing bowl. 3. In another mixing bowl, stir together the eggs and coconut oil. Add the wet mixture to the dry mixture. 4. Mix in the remaining ingredients and stir until a soft dough forms. 5. Drop about 2 tablespoons of dough on the baking paper for each cookie and flatten each biscuit until it's 1 inch thick. 6. Bake for about 25 minutes until the cookies are golden and firm to the touch. Remove from the basket to a plate. Let the cookies cool to room temperature and serve.

Gluten-Free Spice Cookies

Prep time: 10 minutes | Cook time: 12 minutes | Serves 4

4 tablespoons unsalted butter, at room temperature	2 teaspoons ground ginger
	1 teaspoon ground cinnamon
2 tablespoons agave nectar	½ teaspoon freshly grated nutmeg
1 large egg	
2 tablespoons water	1 teaspoon baking soda
240 g almond flour	¼ teaspoon kosher, or coarse sea salt
100 g granulated sugar	

1. Line the bottom of the air fryer basket with baking paper cut to fit. 2. In a large bowl, using a hand mixer, beat together the butter, agave, egg, and water on medium speed until light and fluffy. 3. Add the almond flour, sugar, ginger, cinnamon, nutmeg, baking soda, and salt. Beat on low speed until well combined. 4. Roll the dough into 2-tablespoon balls and arrange them on the baking paper in the basket. (They don't really spread too much but try to leave a little room between them.) Set the air fryer to 164ºC, and cook for 12 minutes, or until the tops of cookies are lightly browned. 5. Transfer to a wire rack and let cool completely. Store in an airtight container for up to a week.

Coconut-Custard Pie

Prep time: 10 minutes | Cook time: 20 to 23 minutes
| Serves 4

240 ml milk	2 eggs
50 g granulated sugar, plus 2 tablespoons	2 tablespoons melted butter
	Cooking spray
30 g scone mix	50 g desiccated, sweetened coconut
1 teaspoon vanilla extract	

1. Place all ingredients except coconut in a medium bowl. 2. Using a hand mixer, beat on high speed for 3 minutes. 3. Let sit for 5 minutes. 4. Preheat the air fryer to 164ºC. 5. Spray a baking pan with cooking spray and place pan in air fryer basket. 6. Pour filling into pan and sprinkle coconut over top. 7. Cook pie for 20 to 23 minutes or until center sets.

Chocolate Peppermint Cheesecake

Prep time: 5 minutes | Cook time: 18 minutes | Serves 6

Crust:
110 g butter, melted
55 g coconut flour
2 tablespoons granulated sweetener
Cooking spray
Topping:

110 g unsweetened cooking chocolate
180 g mascarpone cheese, at room temperature
1 teaspoon vanilla extract
2 drops peppermint extract

1. Preheat the air fryer to 176°C. Lightly coat a baking pan with cooking spray. 2. In a mixing bowl, whisk together the butter, flour, and sweetener until well combined. Transfer the mixture to the prepared baking pan. 3. Place the baking pan in the air fryer and bake for 18 minutes until a toothpick inserted in the center comes out clean. 4. Remove the crust from the air fryer to a wire rack to cool. 5. Once cooled completely, place it in the freezer for 20 minutes. 6. When ready, combine all the ingredients for the topping in a small bowl and stir to incorporate. 7. Spread this topping over the crust and let it sit for another 15 minutes in the freezer. 8. Serve chilled.

Lemon Curd Pavlova

Prep time: 10 minutes | Cook time: 1 hour | Serves 4

Shell:
3 large egg whites
¼ teaspoon cream of tartar
75 g powdered sweetener
1 teaspoon grated lemon zest
1 teaspoon lemon extract
Lemon Curd:

100 g powdered sweetener
120 ml lemon juice
4 large eggs
120 ml coconut oil
For Garnish (Optional):
Blueberries
powdered sweetener

1. Preheat the air fryer to 135°C. Thoroughly grease a pie pan with butter or coconut oil. 2. Make the shell: In a small bowl, use a hand mixer to beat the egg whites and cream of tartar until soft peaks form. With the mixer on low, slowly sprinkle in the sweetener and mix until it's completely incorporated. 3. Add the lemon zest and lemon extract and continue to beat with the hand mixer until stiff peaks form. 4. Spoon the mixture into the greased pie pan, then smooth it across the bottom, up the sides, and onto the rim to form a shell. Bake for 1 hour, then turn off the air fryer and let the shell stand in the air fryer for 20 minutes. (The shell can be made up to 3 days ahead and stored in an airtight container in the refrigerator, if desired.) 5. While the shell bakes, make the lemon curd: In a medium-sized heavy-bottomed saucepan, whisk together the sweetener, lemon juice, and eggs. Add the coconut oil and place the pan on the stovetop over medium heat. Once the oil is melted, whisk constantly until the mixture thickens and thickly coats the back of a spoon, about 10 minutes. Do not allow the mixture to come to a boil. 6. Pour the lemon curd mixture through a fine-mesh strainer into a medium-sized bowl. Place the bowl inside a larger bowl filled with ice water and whisk occasionally until the curd is completely cool, about 15 minutes. 7. Place the lemon curd on top of the shell and garnish with blueberries and powdered sweetener, if desired. Store leftovers in the refrigerator for up to 4 days.

Pineapple Wontons

Prep time: 15 minutes | Cook time: 15 to 18 minutes per batch | Serves 5

225 g cream cheese
170 g finely chopped fresh pineapple

20 wonton wrappers
Cooking oil spray

1. In a small microwave-safe bowl, heat the cream cheese in the microwave on high power for 20 seconds to soften. 2. In a medium bowl, stir together the cream cheese and pineapple until mixed well. 3. Lay out the wonton wrappers on a work surface. A clean table or large cutting board works well. 4. Spoon 1½ teaspoons of the cream cheese mixture onto each wrapper. Be careful not to overfill. 5. Fold each wrapper diagonally across to form a triangle. Bring the 2 bottom corners up toward each other. Do not close the wrapper yet. Bring up the 2 open sides and push out any air. Squeeze the open edges together to seal. 6. Insert the crisper plate into the basket and the basket into the unit. Preheat the air fryer to 200°C. 7. Once the unit is preheated, spray the crisper plate with cooking oil. Place the wontons into the basket. You can work in batches or stack the wontons. Spray the wontons with the cooking oil. 8. Cook wontons for 10 minutes, then remove the basket, flip each wonton, and spray them with more oil. Reinsert the basket to resume cooking for 5 to 8 minutes more until the wontons are light golden brown and crisp. 9. If cooking in batches, remove the cooked wontons from the basket and repeat steps 7 and 8 for the remaining wontons. 10. When the cooking is complete, cool for 5 minutes before serving.

Chocolate Croissants

Prep time: 5 minutes | Cook time: 24 minutes | Serves 8

1 sheet frozen puff pastry, thawed

100 g chocolate-hazelnut spread
1 large egg, beaten

1. On a lightly floured surface, roll puff pastry into a 14-inch square. Cut pastry into quarters to form 4 squares. Cut each square diagonally to form 8 triangles. 2. Spread 2 teaspoons chocolate-hazelnut spread on each triangle; from wider end, roll up pastry. Brush egg on top of each roll. 3. Preheat the air fryer to 192°C. Air fry rolls in batches, 3 or 4 at a time, 8 minutes per batch, or until pastry is golden brown. 4. Cool on a wire rack; serve while warm or at room temperature.

Blackberry Cobbler

Prep time: 15 minutes | Cook time: 25 to 30 minutes | Serves 6

330 g fresh or frozen blackberries	1 teaspoon vanilla extract
350 g granulated sugar, divided into 200 g and 150 g	8 tablespoons butter, melted
	125 g self-raising flour
	1 to 2 tablespoons oil

1. In a medium bowl, stir together the blackberries, 200 g of sugar, and vanilla. 2. In another medium bowl, stir together the melted butter, remaining 150 g of sugar, and flour until a dough forms. 3. Spritz a baking pan with oil. Add the blackberry mixture. Crumble the flour mixture over the fruit. Cover the pan with aluminum foil. 4. Preheat the air fryer to 176°C. 5. Place the covered pan in the air fryer basket. Cook for 20 to 25 minutes until the filling is thickened. 6. Uncover the pan and cook for 5 minutes more, depending on how juicy and browned you like your cobbler. Let sit for 5 minutes before serving.

Almond-Roasted Pears

Prep time: 10 minutes | Cook time: 15 to 20 minutes | Serves 4

Yogurt Topping:	2 whole pears
140-170 g pot vanilla Greek yogurt	4 crushed Biscoff biscuits
¼ teaspoon almond flavoring	1 tablespoon flaked almonds
	1 tablespoon unsalted butter

1. Stir the almond flavoring into yogurt and set aside while preparing pears. 2. Halve each pear and spoon out the core. 3. Place pear halves in air fryer basket, skin side down. 4. Stir together the crushed biscuits and almonds. Place a quarter of this mixture into the hollow of each pear half. 5. Cut butter into 4 pieces and place one piece on top of biscuit mixture in each pear. 6. Roast at 184°C for 15 to 20 minutes, or until pears have cooked through but are still slightly firm. 7. Serve pears warm with a dollop of yogurt topping.

Oatmeal Raisin Bars

Prep time: 15 minutes | Cook time: 15 minutes | Serves 8

40 g plain flour	50 g granulated sugar
¼ teaspoon kosher, or coarse sea salt	120 ml canola, or rapeseed oil
¼ teaspoon baking powder	1 large egg
¼ teaspoon ground cinnamon	1 teaspoon vanilla extract
50 g light brown sugar, lightly packed	110 g quick-cooking oats
	60 g raisins

1. Preheat the air fryer to 184°C. 2. In a large bowl, combine the plain flour, kosher salt, baking powder, ground cinnamon, light brown sugar, granulated sugar, canola oil, egg, vanilla extract, quick-cooking oats, and raisins. 3. Spray a baking pan with nonstick cooking spray, then pour the oat mixture into the pan and press down to evenly distribute. Place the pan in the air fryer and bake for 15 minutes or until golden brown. 4. Remove from the air fryer and allow to cool in the pan on a wire rack for 20 minutes before slicing and serving.

Apple Wedges with Apricots

Prep time: 5 minutes | Cook time: 15 to 18 minutes | Serves 4

4 large apples, peeled and sliced into 8 wedges	1 to 2 tablespoons granulated sugar
2 tablespoons light olive oil	½ teaspoon ground cinnamon
95 g dried apricots, chopped	

1. Preheat the air fryer to 180°C. 2. Toss the apple wedges with the olive oil in a mixing bowl until well coated. 3. Place the apple wedges in the air fryer basket and air fry for 12 to 15 minutes. 4. Sprinkle with the dried apricots and air fry for another 3 minutes. 5. Meanwhile, thoroughly combine the sugar and cinnamon in a small bowl. 6. Remove the apple wedges from the basket to a plate. Serve sprinkled with the sugar mixture.

Indian Toast and Milk

Prep time: 10 minutes | Cook time: 20 minutes | Serves 4

305 g sweetened, condensed milk	4 slices white bread
240 ml evaporated milk	2 to 3 tablespoons ghee or butter, softened
240 ml single cream	2 tablespoons crushed pistachios, for garnish (optional)
1 teaspoon ground cardamom, plus additional for garnish	
1 pinch saffron threads	

1. In a baking pan, combine the condensed milk, evaporated milk, half-and-half, cardamom, and saffron. Stir until well combined. 2. Place the pan in the air fryer basket. Set the air fryer to 176°C for 15 minutes, stirring halfway through the cooking time. Remove the sweetened milk from the air fryer and set aside. 3. Cut each slice of bread into two triangles. Brush each side with ghee. Place the bread in the air fryer basket. Keeping the air fryer on 176°C cook for 5 minutes or until golden brown and toasty. 4. Remove the bread from the air fryer. Arrange two triangles in each of four wide, shallow bowls. Pour the hot milk mixture on top of the bread and let soak for 30 minutes. 5. Garnish with pistachios if using, and sprinkle with additional cardamom.

Pumpkin-Spice Bread Pudding

Prep time: 15 minutes | Cook time: 35 minutes | Serves 6

Bread Pudding:	1/3 loaf of day-old baguette or
175 ml heavy whipping cream	crusty country bread, cubed
120 g canned pumpkin	4 tablespoons unsalted butter,
80 ml whole milk	melted
65 g granulated sugar	Sauce:
1 large egg plus 1 yolk	80 ml pure maple syrup
½ teaspoon pumpkin pie spice	1 tablespoon unsalted butter
⅛ teaspoon kosher, or coarse	120 ml heavy whipping cream
sea salt	½ teaspoon pure vanilla extract

1. For the bread pudding: In a medium bowl, combine the cream, pumpkin, milk, sugar, egg and yolk, pumpkin pie spice, and salt. Whisk until well combined. 2. In a large bowl, toss the bread cubes with the melted butter. Add the pumpkin mixture and gently toss until the ingredients are well combined. 3. Transfer the mixture to a baking pan. Place the pan in the air fryer basket. Set the fryer to 176°C cooking for 35 minutes, or until custard is set in the middle. 4. Meanwhile, for the sauce: In a small saucepan, combine the syrup and butter. Heat over medium heat, stirring, until the butter melts. Stir in the cream and simmer, stirring often, until the sauce has thickened, about 15 minutes. Stir in the vanilla. Remove the pudding from the air fryer. 5. Let the pudding stand for 10 minutes before serving with the warm sauce.

Ricotta Lemon Poppy Seed Cake

Prep time: 10 minutes | Cook time: 55 minutes | Serves 4

Unsalted butter, at room	55 g coconut oil, melted
temperature	2 tablespoons poppy seeds
110 g almond flour	1 teaspoon baking powder
100 g granulated sugar	1 teaspoon pure lemon extract
3 large eggs	Grated zest and juice of 1
55 g heavy cream	lemon, plus more zest for
60 g full-fat ricotta cheese	garnish

1. Generously butter a baking pan. Line the bottom of the pan with baking paper cut to fit. 2. In a large bowl, combine the almond flour, sugar, eggs, cream, ricotta, coconut oil, poppy seeds, baking powder, lemon extract, lemon zest, and lemon juice. Beat with a hand mixer on medium speed, until well blended and fluffy. 3. Pour the batter into the prepared pan. Cover the pan tightly with aluminum foil. Set the pan in the air fryer basket. Set the air fryer to 164°C and cook for 45 minutes. Remove the foil and cook for 10 to 15 minutes more, until a knife (do not use a toothpick) inserted into the center of the cake comes out clean. 4. Let the cake cool in the pan on a wire rack for 10 minutes. Remove the cake from pan and let it cool on the rack for 15 minutes before slicing. 5. Top with additional lemon zest, slice and serve.

Shortcut Spiced Apple Butter

Prep time: 5 minutes | Cook time: 1 hour | Makes 1¼ cups

Cooking spray	½ teaspoon kosher, or coarse
500 g store-bought unsweetened	sea salt
applesauce	¼ teaspoon ground cinnamon
130 g packed light brown sugar	⅛ teaspoon ground allspice
3 tablespoons fresh lemon juice	

1. Spray a cake pan with cooking spray. Whisk together all the ingredients in a bowl until smooth, then pour into the greased pan. Set the pan in the air fryer and bake at 172°C until the apple mixture is caramelized, reduced to a thick purée, and fragrant, about 1 hour. 2. Remove the pan from the air fryer, stir to combine the caramelized bits at the edge with the rest, then let cool completely to thicken. Scrape the apple butter into a jar and store in the refrigerator for up to 2 weeks.

Olive Oil Cake

Prep time: 10 minutes | Cook time: 30 minutes | Serves 8

120 g blanched finely ground	75 g granulated sweetener
almond flour	1 teaspoon vanilla extract
5 large eggs, whisked	1 teaspoon baking powder
175 ml extra-virgin olive oil	

1. In a large bowl, mix all ingredients. Pour batter into an ungreased round nonstick baking dish. 2. Place dish into air fryer basket. Adjust the temperature to 148°C and bake for 30 minutes. The cake will be golden on top and firm in the center when done. 3. Let cake cool in dish 30 minutes before slicing and serving.

Almond Shortbread

Prep time: 10 minutes | Cook time: 12 minutes | Serves 8

110 g unsalted butter	1 teaspoon pure almond extract
100 g granulated sugar	125 g plain flour

1. In bowl of a stand mixer fitted with the paddle attachment, beat the butter and sugar on medium speed until light and fluffy (3 to 4 minutes). Add the almond extract and beat until combined (about 30 seconds). Turn the mixer to low. Add the flour a little at a time and beat for about 2 minutes more until well-incorporated. 2. Pat the dough into an even layer in a baking pan. Place the pan in the air fryer basket. Set the air fryer to 192°C and bake for 12 minutes. 3. Carefully remove the pan from air fryer basket. While the shortbread is still warm and soft, cut it into 8 wedges. 4. Let cool in the pan on a wire rack for 5 minutes. Remove the wedges from the pan and let cool completely on the rack before serving.

Grilled Pineapple Dessert

Prep time: 5 minutes | Cook time: 12 minutes | Serves 4

Coconut, or avocado oil for misting, or cooking spray
4½-inch-thick slices fresh pineapple, core removed
1 tablespoon honey

¼ teaspoon brandy, or apple juice
2 tablespoons slivered almonds, toasted
Vanilla frozen yogurt, coconut sorbet, or ice cream

1. Spray both sides of pineapple slices with oil or cooking spray. Place into air fryer basket. 2. Air fry at 200ºC for 6 minutes. Turn slices over and cook for an additional 6 minutes. 3. Mix together the honey and brandy. 4. Remove cooked pineapple slices from air fryer, sprinkle with toasted almonds, and drizzle with honey mixture. 5. Serve with a scoop of frozen yogurt or sorbet on the side.

Caramelized Fruit Skewers

Prep time: 10 minutes | Cook time: 3 to 5 minutes | Serves 4

2 peaches, peeled, pitted, and thickly sliced
3 plums, halved and pitted
3 nectarines, halved and pitted
1 tablespoon honey
½ teaspoon ground cinnamon

¼ teaspoon ground allspice
Pinch cayenne pepper
Special Equipment:
8 metal skewers

1. Preheat the air fryer to 204ºC. 2. Thread, alternating peaches, plums, and nectarines, onto the metal skewers that fit into the air fryer. 3. Thoroughly combine the honey, cinnamon, allspice, and cayenne in a small bowl. Brush the glaze generously over the fruit skewers. 4. Transfer the fruit skewers to the air fryer basket. You may need to cook in batches to avoid overcrowding. 5. Air fry for 3 to 5 minutes, or until the fruit is caramelized. 6. Remove from the basket and repeat with the remaining fruit skewers. 7. Let the fruit skewers rest for 5 minutes before serving.

Printed in Great Britain
by Amazon

20314268R00041